ABERDEEN FC
On This Day

ABERDEEN FC
On This Day

History, Facts & Figures
from Every Day of the Year

KEVIN STIRLING

ABERDEEN FC
On This Day

History, Facts & Figures from Every Day of the Year

All statistics, facts and figures are correct as of 31st August 2008

© Kevin Stirling

Kevin Stirling has asserted his rights in accordance with the Copyright, Designs and Patents Act 1988 to be identified as the author of this work.

Published By:
Pitch Publishing Ltd,
A2 Yeoman Gate,
Durrington BN13 3QZ

Email: info@pitchpublishing.co.uk
Web: www.pitchpublishing.co.uk

First published 2008
Reprinted 2015

A catalogue record for this book is available from the British Library

10-digit ISBN: 1-9054112-4-3
13-digit ISBN: 978-1-9054112-4-5
Printed and bound in Great Britain by TJ International

To my late friend John Hepburn;
a true Aberdeen supporter,
Stand Free forever.

Kevin Stirling – September 2008

ACKNOWLEDGEMENTS

First of all my sincere thanks to my wife Bernadette and children Joanne and Kevin; they have had to put up with my usual moans and groans on occasion. Thanks also to Bob Stewart at the Aberdeen Journals library for his help in tracking down that elusive photo. Thanks also to Aberdeen Journals themselves for permission to tap into their superb archive. Thanks to Pitch Publishing and Dan Tester for initially inviting me to join their growing team and also their smooth approach to the editing process. Thanks also to Aberdeen FC and Duncan Fraser for their backing with this project; hopefully the book will do justice to a great football club.

FOREWORD BY WILLIE MILLER

Having played for Aberdeen for the best part of twenty years I have come to appreciate more than most just what it means to play for the club and be part of the Dons' rich history. I was lucky enough to captain Aberdeen through the late 1970s and 1980s when we brought so much success to the club, carving out our own piece of Aberdeen FC history. Kevin has once again brought Dons history to life with his latest effort, full of unique facts and figures on the club. Apart from those heady days of the 1980s, reading through the book only brings home to you that there is so much more to the club than what we achieved.

Our success at home and in Europe was a fantastic time for all Aberdeen players and supporters, but it was interesting to read about the lean times as well. The early days of the club are well covered and offer a fascinating insight on the club. It has been a pleasure to be a part of the wonderful history of Aberdeen Football Club. I trust you will enjoy reading Kevin's latest work as much as I did.

Willie Miller, Aberdeen FC 1972-90 and 1992-95

INTRODUCTION

'Aberdeen: On This Day' looks back on the rich history of Aberdeen Football Club, charting the many highs and considerable lows that the club have endured through the years.

While the present Aberdeen came into being in 1903, football in the north-east of Scotland began some 22 years previously and many of the fascinating events during that period are covered. Documenting the Dons' history in diary form threw up some unique events that happened on the same date. Aberdeen supporters will forever hold the 11th May very dear to them as that was the day the club enjoyed their finest hour when they defeated the mighty Real Madrid to lift the European Cup Winners' Cup.

On that same date in 1991 it was perhaps the Dons darkest hour as they lost to bitter rivals Rangers on the final day of the season to effectively throw away a great opportunity to clinch the league title. Those stark contrasts in fortunes are all part of Aberdeen FC history: for instance, on the same day in January Aberdeen's long sequence of not losing a goal came to an end in 1971 while 17 years later record signing Charlie Nicholas made his home debut for the club. The real contrast came on the 10th February as Aberdeen recorded their highest ever victory with a 13-0 hammering of Peterhead in a 1923 Scottish Cup tie. Forty two years later lowly East Fife humbled Aberdeen in the same competition in what was arguably their worst result in the competition's history.

There are also some fascinating stories to tell about some of the lesser known Aberdeen players. While club legends like Miller, McLeish, Leighton, Harper, Strachan, Armstrong, Mills and many others are well covered in this book, there is also the tale of the grandly named Lachlan McMillan; signed from Hearts to help Aberdeen defeat Partick in a Cup-tie. McMillan scored and he and Benny Yorston were carried shoulder high on their return to Aberdeen. In the next round he broke his leg against Dundee after two minutes and his 11-day career at Pittodrie was over.

There are many more such stories to tell and hopefully you will enjoy reading them as much as I have done pulling it all together.

Kevin Stirling, September 2008

ABERDEEN FC
On This Day

JANUARY

TUESDAY 1st JANUARY 1889

Aberdeen played two games on the same day to bring in the New Year. First up was Glasgow club Kings Park who defeated an Aberdeen-select 8-1. The afternoon match was against a Hampden XI and most of the Dons players were put through their paces again and went down 6-1 to the visitors. Both matches were played in the Chanonry, the original Aberdeen ground in Old Aberdeen.

SATURDAY 1st JANUARY 1949

Jackie Hather and Chris Anderson made their first team debuts for Aberdeen against Dundee at Pittodrie. Hather was the only Englishman in the Dons side that won the championship in 1955. Regarded as the quickest player in Scotland at that time, Hather was also hampered by a medical condition in that he played his entire career with one kidney.

MONDAY 1st JANUARY 1945

Hungarian international Zoltan Varga was born in Val, Hungary. Varga was a controversial character in many ways but nonetheless a highly-gifted footballer who made a lasting impression during his short Aberdeen career in 1972.

MONDAY 1st JANUARY 1951

Billed as the match of the season, the visit of league leaders Dundee to Pittodrie on New Years' Day attracted a crowd of 30,000 to see if Aberdeen could take over at the top at Dundee's expense. Fred Martin was missing through injury which offered a rare start for reserve goalkeeper Hugh Curran. In a tense match of few chances, it was George Hamilton who squeezed the ball past Lynch from Delaney's corner to give Aberdeen a memorable victory.

FRIDAY 1st JANUARY 1971

Arthur Graham was on target for Aberdeen as they welcomed traditional New Year opponents Dundee to Pittodrie. With only one defeat from 18 league games, Aberdeen were making a serious challenge to Celtic's perceived dominance of the league. Goals from Tom McMillan and Steve Murray helped Aberdeen to a 3-0 win that led to the players receiving a standing ovation from the 24,000 crowd.

THURSDAY 2ND JANUARY 1902

Kilmarnock made the long trip north in the New Year to play Aberdeen side Victoria United in a friendly. Victoria United were based in the south side of the city and defeated the Ayrshire club 2-0 before a 1,000 crowd at their Central Park home.

THURSDAY 2ND JANUARY 1947

A day after losing to Falkirk at home, Aberdeen travelled to Celtic Park and won 5-1, their biggest ever win against Celtic in Glasgow. George Hamilton was the Dons tormentor-in-chief as he became the only Aberdeen player to score four at Parkhead. Hamilton hit three second half goals as the Dons blitzed their hosts. The game also marked a debut for goalkeeper Frank Watson who tragically died at a young age in 1953.

WEDNESDAY 2ND JANUARY 1952

Bogey side East Fife arrived at Pittodrie and after three straight defeats the Dons got their season back on track with a 2-1 win over the Methil side. The highlight of the game for the 20,000 crowd was a sublime winner from George Hamilton in the 87th minute. Hamilton had taken the ball from his own half to slide it past Curran in the East Fife goal.

WEDNESDAY 2ND JANUARY 1957

Aberdeen continued their fine festive form with a 2-1 win at Partick Thistle although their appalling injury woes continued. This time it was Allan Boyd who was carried off after knee ligament damage and he would not play again all season. Jackie Hather scored the winner in 44 minutes before a 10,000 Firhill crowd.

THURSDAY 2ND JANUARY 1958

Jim Bonthrone, who went on to manage Aberdeen in the 1970s, was a surprise goalscorer against the Dons for East Fife as the Methil club were the Reds' first visitors in 1958. An even first half gave way to the Dons hitting four second half goals, three coming from Jackie Hather in a 6-2 win.

MONDAY 3ʀᴅ JANUARY 1910

Ireland international Charlie O'Hagan was on target for Aberdeen as they were held to a 1-1 draw against Partick Thistle at Pittodrie. Aberdeen had drawn against Dundee in the New Year fixture and were left frustrated again as the Firhill side kept the Aberdeen forwards at bay. It was a busy time for Aberdeen as they were due to play Dundee again a day later in Willie Lennie's benefit match.

MONDAY 3ʀᴅ JANUARY 1977

One of the finest displays from Joe Harper as he helped Aberdeen to a 4-1 win over Hearts at Pittodrie before a New Year crowd of 18,800. The pitch was rock hard from the frosty conditions and Harper was at his best as he led a cumbersome Hearts defence a merry dance. The pick of his three goals was a superb balancing act in the box as he slipped past two defenders and beat Cruickshank from close range.

MONDAY 3ʀᴅ JANUARY 1983

Dundee United may have been title pretenders but not for the first time that season they were torn apart in front of their own support by a slick Aberdeen side. It was also United's first defeat at home since May 1982, when it was the Reds who were last to win there. On this occasion the 3-0 win did not flatter the Dons; they were so far ahead that Aberdeen had scored eight of the 14 goals that United had conceded so far that season.

TUESDAY 4ᴛʜ JANUARY 1910

Willie Lennie became the first Aberdeen player to receive a testimonial from the club. Lennie had been regarded as a bit of a nomad in his football career but it was at Pittodrie that he finally settled to play the best football of his career. Dundee were among the list of his former clubs and they came north to pay tribute. Aberdeen won 3-2 before a 4,000 crowd.

WEDNESDAY 4TH JANUARY 1911

Donald Colman was awarded a benefit match by the club after becoming the oldest Aberdeen player to be capped for Scotland at the age of 33. Colman joined Aberdeen from Motherwell in 1907 he went on to enjoy a long association with the club that concluded with him being the club trainer in the 1930s. Dundee travelled north for Colman's testimonial game and more than 5,000 turned out to see Aberdeen win 4-2 with Colman missing a penalty. He was guaranteed £200 from the match and was also responsible for bringing a new concept to British football with Pittodrie having the first dugout in Britain after he had taken the idea from Norway during one of his summer coaching trips.

SATURDAY 4TH JANUARY 1969

Aberdeen were languishing in 14th place as they faced Dundee United. Despite some woeful form in recent weeks, the Reds turned in one of their best performances of the season in a 4-1 win before 15,000 fans. After Cameron missed a penalty with the Dons 2-0 ahead, the visitors completed a surprise victory. Henning Boel made his debut in the Aberdeen defence.

MONDAY 5TH JANUARY 1903

The Scottish League dashed hopes of Aberdeen being admitted into the league after it admitted that 'drastic changes would have to be made to the constitution' before the club would be considered to join the professional ranks.

WEDNESDAY 5TH JANUARY 1938

Dave Halliday was appointed Aberdeen manager after he was successful from a list of 100 applicants. Halliday had been winding down his playing career with Yeovil Town and he was the surprise choice to take over from Pat Travers.

SATURDAY 5TH JANUARY 1957

Despite a growing injury list, the Dons completed a three-game festive spell with a third victory; this time the 4-0 win over St Mirren had hauled Aberdeen into the top six. Hughie Hay scored twice before a 13,000 crowd.

SATURDAY 5TH JANUARY 1991

Eoin Jess was inspired as he set about a one-man demolition job of Dunfermline at East End Park. Aberdeen were looking to keep their title challenge going over the festive period and young Jess scored all four Dons goals in a 4-1 win.

SATURDAY 6TH JANUARY 1962

Stirling Albion had been on the end of several heavy defeats from Aberdeen in recent years but they extracted a small measure of revenge in a surprise 3-0 win at Annfield. Conditions were far from ideal as both sets of players and officials protested to the referee before the game that it should not go ahead. However, referee Phillips decided the pitch was 'playable' and the home side eased to a win that eased their relegation fears.

SATURDAY 7TH JANUARY 1911

Aberdeen's title hopes were given a blow following a disappointing 1-1 draw against Falkirk at Brockville. The 'Bairns' were surprising challengers at the top end of the table but it was Rangers and Aberdeen that would battle it out for the championship. Angus McIntosh scored for the Dons before 7,000 supporters.

TUESDAY 9TH JANUARY 1940

A tragic day for Aberdeen as popular South African player Herbert Currer was on board the Dunbar Castle ship as it struck a German mine off the south coast of England. Originally from Transvaal, Currer had been with the successful Arcadia side in South Africa before moving to Scotland to join Aberdeen.

SATURDAY 10TH JANUARY 1970

Rare starts for Sutherland and Kirkland in the Aberdeen defence as struggling Raith Rovers were on the end of a heavy 5-1 defeat after Ernie McGarr had gifted the Kirkcaldy side an early lead. Joe Harper continued to build his growing reputation as news that dropped goalkeeper Bobby Clark was on the verge of signing for Rangers. With both Clark and McGarr on their books, the goalkeeping position at Pittodrie was a healthy one.

SUNDAY 11th JANUARY 1948

Joe Harper, the Aberdeen record goalscorer, was born in Greenock. Harper joined the Dons in October 1969 and went on to become the only player to score more than 200 goals for the club in his two spells at Pittodrie. Known by the support as 'King Joey', he attained legendary status by a generation of Aberdeen supporters. After moving to Everton in December 1972, Harper eventually returned for a successful second spell with the club in March 1976. Joe went on to win all three domestic winners medals with the Dons, before retiring in 1981.

SATURDAY 11th JANUARY 1964

Fog descended on Pittodrie for a classic Scottish Cup tie that had the 15,500 crowd giving young forward Ernie Winchester a standing ovation at the end of the game. The Dons had previously lost to Hibernian in the League Cup at Pittodrie and after racing into a 4-0 lead, they were pegged back and hanging on as Hibernian managed to get two goals back. Enter Ernie Winchester who powered a Kerrigan cross into the net to put Aberdeen through to the next round.

SATURDAY 11th JANUARY 1992

Hearts had emerged as surprise challengers for the title but they were torn apart by an Aberdeen side that had been struggling for form. Eoin Jess and Scott Booth gave the Hearts defence a torrid time of it as the Dons ran out convincing 4-0 winners before a 16,291 Tynecastle crowd.

SATURDAY 12th JANUARY 1901

Orion made the long trek to Ayrshire to take on Ayr United in a Scottish Cup tie at Somerset Park. The Aberdeen side were given little hope of taking anything from the game but came away with a 3-3 draw to take the tie back to Aberdeen. The replay at Cattofield a week later attracted a 3,500 crowd as Ayr progressed to the next round after a 3-1 win.

SATURDAY 12TH JANUARY 1980

A crucial win for Aberdeen against Rangers at Pittodrie as a late goal from Derek Hamilton gave the Dons a 3-2 win. Gordon Strachan had put the Reds ahead but Rangers fought back to take the lead early in the second period through Colin Jackson. It was Hamilton who set up Steve Archibald to level and then he went on to score a dramatic winner in the final minute. Aberdeen still trailed leaders Celtic by 10 points…

SATURDAY 13TH JANUARY 1951

With Celtic still in contention for the championship, the Dons' 4-3 win over the Parkhead side was Aberdeen's fourth consecutive win over the Old Firm that season. Despite Celtic racing into a two-goal lead after 16 minutes, the Reds clawed their way back into the game. By the time that Don Emery crashed home a penalty in 79 minutes, Aberdeen were 4-2 ahead.

SATURDAY 13TH JANUARY 1990

Aberdeen recovered from a defeat at Ibrox by beating Dunfermline Athletic 4-1 in a convincing win at Pittodrie. Hans Gillhaus was again missing through injury but Charlie Nicholas was paired up front with League Cup hero Paul Mason and both scored for the Dons before a 14,000 crowd.

SATURDAY 14TH JANUARY 1899

Orion, one of the founder members of the present Aberdeen FC, welcomed Kilmarnock to their Cattofield ground for a Scottish Cup tie. It was a first visit north for the Ayrshire side and the Central Park ground was full, with both the stand and enclosure packed with supporters. Kilmarnock won 2-0 while at Montrose Aberdeen, were losing 4-0 at the Links in the Northern League.

WEDNESDAY 14TH JANUARY 1970

Joe Harper was in the Scotland under-23 side that drew 1-1 with Wales at Pittodrie in a game that was played in dreadful weather. Former Don Frank Munro was also in the side as John O'Hare scored the Scots goal before a 15,349 crowd that braved the Arctic conditions.

FRANK MUNRO WATCHES AS LORIMER'S SHOT HITS THE POST AGAINST WALES UNDER-23'S AT PITTODRIE IN 1970

SATURDAY 14TH JANUARY 1978

A fourth consecutive defeat for Celtic saw the Parkhead side drop into the relegation zone as Aberdeen maintained their challenge to Rangers at the top. The Dons 2-1 win, before a capacity 24,600 attendance, came from two strikes by Dom Sullivan. Celtic missed a late penalty through Lynch when his effort came back off the post.

WEDNESDAY 15TH JANUARY 2003

Darren Mackie scored the Dons goal in a friendly against Ajax of Holland. The game was played near to the Dons training camp in Portugal as the squad took advantage of the mid-winter break. Aberdeen gave a good account of themselves but were beaten 2-1.

SATURDAY 16TH JANUARY 1932

A real shock for Aberdeen as they were sent crashing out of the Scottish Cup at lowly Arbroath in the first round. Although conditions at Gayfield were not ideal, Aberdeen looked to be heading through after Matt Armstrong scored in 41 minutes. However, two second period goals from Harry Oliphant – previously discarded by Aberdeen – put the Dons out. Watching in the 4,000 crowd was Harry Lauder, the famed Scots comedian. The laughs that day were on Aberdeen.

SATURDAY 16TH JANUARY 1971

When Pat Stanton scored for Hibernian in the 64th minute at Easter Road it ended the Dons' record sequence of 15 straight wins, the last 12 without conceding a single goal. The last time Bobby Clark conceded a goal was against St Mirren in October. Aberdeen had gone 1,155 minutes without losing a goal as they climbed to the top of the league.

SATURDAY 16TH JANUARY 1988

More than 20,000 turned out for the Dons game against Dunfermline Athletic at Pittodrie to see the home debut of Charlie Nicholas. The former Celtic star was brought back to Scotland by Ian Porterfield as the Dons broke their club record transfer of £400,000. Aberdeen went on to win 1-0 with Willie Falconer scoring the winner.

SATURDAY 17TH JANUARY 1953

Third Lanark had proven to be a thorn in Aberdeen flesh in recent years, so it was a delighted Dons side that completed a league double over the Cathkin Park outfit with a 1-0 win in Glasgow. Jackie Hater scored the winner after 47 minutes to send Third Lanark to the foot of the table.

SATURDAY 17TH JANUARY 1976

Former Campsie Watch defender Willie Garner made his debut for Aberdeen in a thrilling 3-3 draw against Hearts at Tynecastle. The 10,300 crowd saw the Reds take the lead three times, only to be hauled back by the home side. Andy Geoghegan, deputising for Bobby Clark, saved a penalty from Prentice with the score at 2-1 for Aberdeen.

SATURDAY 18TH JANUARY 1958

Scotland international Peter Weir was born in Renfrewshire. Weir was part of the Aberdeen side that won the European Cup Winners' Cup in 1983. Signed by Alex Ferguson from St Mirren in May 1981, he was the record transfer between two Scottish clubs at the time with a £330,000 deal that also saw Ian Scanlon go to Paisley.

SATURDAY 19TH JANUARY 1929

Non-league side Solway Star visited Pittodrie in the Scottish Cup. Aberdeen eased past the amateur side with a comfortable 5-0 win before a 9,296 crowd. Benny Yorston scored twice and the Aberdeen marksman was also on target in the Dons subsequent ties that season against Queen's Park, Falkirk and St Mirren.

SATURDAY 19TH JANUARY 1957

Norman Davidson scored the only goal of the game to give Aberdeen a welcome win over East Fife at Pittodrie. The game did not lack in controversy as the visitors deployed a frustrating offside trap to spoil the game as a contest. Three Aberdeen goals were disallowed for offside while the one that did slip through was when Davidson looked yards off as he slipped the ball past McCluskey before 14,000 relieved fans.

SATURDAY 19TH JANUARY 1985

Frank McDougall enjoyed his finest hour for Aberdeen as he scored three of the Dons' five goals in their 5-1 mauling of Rangers at Pittodrie. McDougall was a £100,000 signing from St Mirren in 1984 as a direct replacement for Mark McGhee. Before a back injury curtailed his career, Frank was the top scorer in the Premier League in 1985 and also won a clean sweep of domestic winners' medals with the Dons.

MONDAY 20TH JANUARY 1947

Jimmy 'Jinky' Smith was born in Glasgow. Smith joined Aberdeen from Benburb in 1965 as part of the new era under Eddie Turnbull. 'Jinky', as he became known by the Aberdeen support, was one of the most skilful players ever to play for the club. Smith eventually joined Newcastle United for an £80,000 fee in July 1969.

SATURDAY 21ST JANUARY 1899

One of the most keenly-contested clashes in the city was the meeting between Aberdeen and Orion. Due to the dreadful conditions, the scheduled Aberdeenshire Cup semi-final meeting was changed to friendly status and Aberdeen emerged as 6-5 winners. Orion prevailed when the game was played again and went on to lift the trophy after a 5-1 replay win against Victoria United at Cattofield on the 4th March 1899.

WEDNESDAY 21ST JANUARY 1987

Willie Miller scored a rare goal as Aberdeen defeated Hearts 2-1 at Pittodrie. Brian Grant was also on target before a 15,030 crowd. Under new manager Ian Porterfield, the Dons embarked on a 17-game unbeaten run, although several draws frustrated the Dons in what was an exhausting 44-game season.

SATURDAY 22ND JANUARY 1938

Highland League side Elgin City were no match for Aberdeen as the sides clashed in the Scottish Cup. Willie Mills and Billy Strauss showed their class against the part-time side in a comfortable 6-1 win before a crowd of 8,403. Aberdeen went on to lose to East Fife in the third round.

TUESDAY 23RD JANUARY 1962

Leeds United manager Don Revie was an interested spectator in the Pittodrie stands as he cast his eye over Charlie Cooke. Aberdeen were struggling and had not won a home league game for two months. Visitors Raith Rovers looked to be on their way to victory before Cooke scored in a spirited fight-back from the Dons in a 3-3 draw.

SATURDAY 24TH JANUARY 1910

There were chaotic scenes after the Dons' Scottish Cup tie against Cowdenbeath at Central Park. Aberdeen eased past the Fife side with a 1-0 win. The home supporters were none too pleased and at the final whistle several Aberdeen players were attacked by the home supporters.

SATURDAY 25TH JANUARY 1947

Willie Cooper may have been nearing the end of a remarkable 20-year career with Aberdeen but it was his late goal against Partick Thistle at Pittodrie that sent the Dons on their way to Hampden. A crowd of 34,000 witnessed a pulsating cup-tie that looked destined to go to a replay before Cooper stepped up to unleash a 30-yard shot that flew past Thistle goalkeeper Steadward.

SATURDAY 25TH JANUARY 1969

Jim Forrest laid his Berwick Rangers ghosts to rest as his two goals helped Aberdeen to a 3-0 win in the Scottish Cup. Forrest had been in the Rangers side humbled by Berwick in 1967 and was made a scapegoat by the Ibrox club. There was no such shock for Aberdeen, and the 13,600 crowd, as Doug Coutts lined up against his old side as Berwick captain.

MONDAY 25TH JANUARY 1971

Highland League side Elgin City visited Pittodrie for a Scottish Cup tie that had been postponed from the Saturday due to torrential rain. Former Aberdeen captain Ally Shewan was in the visitors' side that were no match for the Dons in a 5-0 win. The 24,136 crowd saw the holders go through to a clash with Dundee United.

SATURDAY 25TH JANUARY 1975

The last Pittodrie crowd in excess of 30,000 turned up for a Scottish Cup tie against Rangers. It took a late goal from Aberdeen captain Willie Miller to force a replay. Rangers took the lead through Ally Scott. Miller was the Dons hero as he made a rare foray into the Rangers half.

THURSDAY 26TH JANUARY 1882

Willie Lennie, the first Aberdeen player to play for Scotland was born in Glasgow. Lennie had the reputation of being something of a football nomad before his arrival at Pittodrie in June 1905. It was at Pittodrie however that he flourished after settling in the north east. After retiring from the game he remained in the Aberdeen area and opened a grocer shop.

SATURDAY 26TH JANUARY 1889

With the city still far removed from the thriving league football in the south, the formation of the Aberdeenshire FA allowed them to set up inter-county matches in the region. An Aberdeen select XI travelled to play Inverness for the inter-county representative match and the game ended in a 2-2 draw before a 2,000 crowd. The Aberdeenshire Association awarded caps to the players who played for the county back then.

SATURDAY 26TH JANUARY 1935

The Dons played their 100th Scottish Cup tie when they travelled to Brockville to face Falkirk. Two goals from Matt Armstrong helped Aberdeen to a 3-2 win before a 14,000 crowd. Aberdeen were eliminated by Hamilton Academical at the semi-final stage that year.

SATURDAY 27TH JANUARY 1900

Local Aberdeen side Orion may have been one of the more ambitious clubs during the late 1890s, but they were humiliated by Kilmarnock in a Scottish Cup tie in Ayrshire. The home side ran out 30-0 winners! It was reported that Orion could not get their usual side together for the long haul to the game and rather than incur a hefty fine from the SFA they travelled down with a scratch team.

SATURDAY 27TH JANUARY 1917

A record defeat for Aberdeen as they were humbled 7-0 against Kilmarnock at Rugby Park. The Dons side was decimated with players missing; eight of the Aberdeen line-up were serving in the military while the trip to Ayrshire was seen as unsafe due to the ongoing hostilities. The train journey was delayed and the players had to get changed on the move. A shadow Aberdeen side, with new faces and trialists, were well beaten against an experienced Kilmarnock side.

SUNDAY 27TH JANUARY 1974

The first-ever official Sunday game in Scotland ended in disappointment for Aberdeen as they went down 2-0 to Dundee in front of 23,574 at Pittodrie in a Scottish Cup tie. Dundee took the lead when Johnston's drive was deflected past Clark.

SATURDAY 28TH JANUARY 1905

Queen's Park came north for a Scottish Cup tie that attracted a record 16,000 crowd to Pittodrie who paid a total of £346 which was also a gate receipt record. In what was Aberdeen's first season in league football, a 2-1 win was another positive step for the club as they looked to gain admission to the top division. In the programme notes for the game it highlighted what was a huge occasion for Aberdeen back then: "Pittodrie today is the scene of a great struggle and it will be remembered as a red-letter day for many years. Queen's arrived last night and were put up in the Douglas Hotel. There was a big crowd at the station to give them a right hearty welcome."

THURSDAY 28TH JANUARY 1915

Willie Mills was born in Alexandria. After joining Aberdeen from Bridgeton Waverley, Mills went on to become a prolific scorer at Pittodrie and he formed a partnership with Matt Armstrong that was one of the most feared in British football. Described by manager Dave Halliday as the 'complete footballer', Mills went on to join Huddersfield Town in 1937.

SATURDAY 28TH JANUARY 1967

Dundee-born Dave Robb made his Aberdeen debut against Dundee at Dens Park in the Scottish Cup. The Dons were inspired by the talented 'Jinky' Smith as he stamped his class all over the game, much to the delight of the sizeable Aberdeen support in the 23,000 crowd. Pick of the goals was Dave Johnston's second as he fired the ball past Arrol on 77 minutes. The Reds went on to win 5-0.

SATURDAY 29TH JANUARY 2000

Hicham Zerouali scored a sensational goal for Aberdeen to take their Scottish Cup tie against St Mirren back to Pittodrie. The goal was also a landmark in Aberdeen history as it was the Dons' 700th in the competition. Zerouali was a Moroccan international who made an immediate impact at the club when he arrived from Fus Rabat. Zerouali went on to score in the replay as the Dons reached the final that season.

SATURDAY 30TH JANUARY 1965

A black day for Aberdeen as they were on the receiving end of their worst defeat in league football as Celtic romped to an 8-0 win. This was also Celtic's first win of the year, and it was John Hughes that mastered the slippery conditions. The Hoops' forward wore sand shoes in the rock hard conditions and helped himself to five goals. This was only the second appearance for the three new Danish signings for the Dons. Jens Petersen, Jorgen Ravn and Leif Mortensen were put through the mill as the Glasgow side announced that Jock Stein was leaving Hibernian to take over at Parkhead.

SATURDAY 31ST JANUARY 1925

Paddy Buckley, the Dons forward who was the top scorer in the championship year of 1955, was born in Leith. Buckley was scoring for fun with St Johnstone in the Second Division before Dave Halliday was the only senior manager willing to take a chance on signing him. It proved to be a masterstroke by Halliday as Buckley went on to become a prolific marksman for the Dons, his 17 goals from 30 league games in 1954/55 helping to bring a first league title to Pittodrie.

ABERDEEN FC
On This Day

FEBRUARY

WEDNESDAY 1st FEBRUARY 1899

Aberdeen left their old ground at the Chanonry in Old Aberdeen to take up the tenancy in what was formerly a dung hill for police horses; Pittodrie or the Gallows Marsh as it was known back then.

SATURDAY 1st FEBRUARY 1947

George Hamilton and Stan Williams scored the goals that gave Aberdeen a 2-1 win over Clyde at Pittodrie to keep the Dons in touch at the top of the table. Incredibly, that game was to be the Dons last league outing for nearly three months as the Reds went on play ten successive Cup matches. After reaching both domestic cup finals the Dons played their final six league games in 21 days.

SATURDAY 2nd FEBRUARY 1907

With the first-team game postponed, the spotlight fell on the Aberdeen reserve side as they went on to win the Aberdeenshire Cup in a 3-1 win over local rivals Harp at Pittodrie. The poor weather conditions did not prevent a 4,000 crowd turning out to see the Dons seconds lift the old trophy.

SATURDAY 2nd FEBRUARY 1991

Scott Booth scored the Dons 1,000th goal since the Premier League began in 1975 as Aberdeen hammered Hearts 5-0 at home to maintain their title challenge. Booth emerged through the youth side at Pittodrie and went on to become a full international for Scotland and also played for European champions Dortmund later in his career. Booth returned to Pittodrie in 2003 after a spell in Holland. He finished as the Dons' top scorer with 10 goals that season.

SATURDAY 3rd FEBRUARY 1900

The first-ever Scotland international in Aberdeen was played when Wales visited Pittodrie. Before a record 11,000 attendance it was reported that trams and carts were ferrying supporters down King Street hours before the game started. Scotland went on to win 5-2 and you could have bought a centre stand seat for the princely sum of two shillings (10p).

WEDNESDAY 3rd FEBRUARY 1960

Brechin City shocked Aberdeen by holding the Dons at Pittodrie in the Scottish Cup. Norman Davidson set the record straight in the replay at Glebe Park as Aberdeen won 6-3 with Davidson scoring five of the Dons goals.

SATURDAY 3rd FEBRUARY 1973

Glebe Park was the venue for a record crowd for Brechin City when Aberdeen visited on Scottish Cup duty. The attendance of 8,123 was made almost entirely of Aberdeen supporters and they were happy to see the Dons go through 4-2 in what was a bruising encounter.

SATURDAY 4th FEBRUARY 1956

The fourth Scottish Cup clash in successive seasons between Rangers and Aberdeen resulted in the Ibrox side gaining revenge for their cup humiliation against the Dons in 1954. The dreadful weather conditions did not prevent the 50,387 Ibrox crowd enjoying another classic. Rangers looked to be heading for the next round after going two goals ahead, but a spirited Aberdeen fight-back saw Graham Leggat score in 80 minutes and a Johnny Allan goal disallowed as the Blues hung on at the end.

SATURDAY 4th FEBRUARY 1967

After picking up only one point from their previous four matches, the Dons got back into European contention with a 5-2 win over bottom club Ayr United at Somerset Park. Reds youngster Dave Robb introduced himself to the side by becoming the 15th Aberdeen booking in recent matches. Bobby Clark saved a last minute penalty from Rutherford by which time Aberdeen had eased to a comfortable win.

SATURDAY 4th FEBRUARY 1984

Aberdeen emerged from the enforced winter break to stretch their lead at the top to six points after a 1-0 win over Celtic at Pittodrie. John Hewitt scored the winner after Bonner could only deflect a Peter Weir shot into his path. The capacity 22,500 crowd saw Jim Leighton save bravely at the feet of Brian McClair to make sure the Dons took full points against their nearest rivals.

SATURDAY 4TH FEBRUARY 1995

A dark day for Aberdeen as a 3-1 defeat at Kilmarnock was the end of the road for Willie Miller as Aberdeen manager. The Dons had been languishing at the foot of the table with only five wins in the league all season. Roy Aitken was put in temporary charge as the Dons looked for an escape route to save their season.

FRIDAY 5TH FEBRUARY 1971

Disaster for the club as fire broke out at Pittodrie. With the stadium empty it was believed a discarded cigarette inside the Main Stand was the cause of a major blaze that ruined all the offices and dressing rooms. The fire also claimed many of the club records and artefacts.

WEDNESDAY 5TH FEBRUARY 1986

With the winners due to face Angus neighbours Arbroath in the next round, Montrose visited Pittodrie in a Scottish Cup tie that was played in blizzard conditions. The Reds eased through with a 4-1 win before a crowd of 8,788 that was dramatically cut due to the poor weather conditions.

MONDAY 6TH FEBRUARY 1899

A meeting of the local council committee agreed to hand over the tenancy of the North Dung Stance to Aberdeen FC on certain conditions which included proper access and various other improvements. Six months later Pittodrie Park was opened after work was completed in laying out a pitch and building an embankment on the south side of the ground.

SATURDAY 6TH FEBRUARY 1960

Drama at Pittodrie as the Dons defeated Celtic 3-2. George Kinnell gave away an early penalty when he thumped Mochan from the back. Kinnell made amends when he equalised after 35 minutes. There was controversy when a Bob Wishart header came off the bar and looked well over the line but the goal was not given. Two minutes from time Ken Brownlee pounced on a slack pass to give Aberdeen the victory.

SATURDAY 7TH FEBRUARY 1948

Nithsdale Wanderers from Dumfries were the Dons opponents in the Scottish Cup. The non-league club from Sanquhar only played the occasional friendly and their tiny Holm Park ground was full for the visit of Aberdeen. Jimmy Stenhouse made his debut for the Dons and scored twice as Aberdeen eased through in a 5-0 win.

SATURDAY 8TH FEBRUARY 1908

A record crowd of 17,000 at Pittodrie turned out for a Scottish Cup tie against Dundee. It was reported that there was great interest in the game in the Aberdeen area with supporters for the first time travelling down from the northern areas in numbers. The receipts amounted to £433, which was the highest on record at that time. The game ended in a 0-0 draw and Aberdeen eventually went through 3-1 after a second replay at Hampden Park.

SATURDAY 9TH FEBRUARY 1907

Disaster for Aberdeen as they were humbled by non-league Johnstone in the Scottish Cup. After a 0-0 draw at Pittodrie, the Renfrew ground was seen by many as unsuitable to host the replay. Aberdeen attempted to get Johnstone to play the second game at Pittodrie and offered a cash incentive. This was turned down after Johnstone insisted on Aberdeen paying them £250 as well as their travel expenses. This was thrown out by the Dons. The game was played in what can be best described as a mud heap and Aberdeen went down 1-0. To add to their humiliation, the Dons lodged a protest over the pitch markings and their protest was thrown out by the SFA.

SATURDAY 9TH FEBRUARY 1952

Kilmarnock made Aberdeen battle all the way in the Scottish Cup at Pittodrie. The Dons received a bye in the first round and before this match a military band played a salute to the late King George. Allan Boyd saved Aberdeen from a difficult replay when he scored the winner in 88 minutes to the delight of the 19,000 crowd.

SATURDAY 9TH FEBRUARY 1957

A 2-2 draw at home to Ayr United was the Dons' first drawn game of the season. Despite going two goals ahead, the Dons slipped up against a side that was destined for relegation. All four goals came in a frantic first half. Aberdeen's miserable afternoon was complete when it emerged that Scotland international Harry Yorston had dislocated an elbow.

SATURDAY 9TH FEBRUARY 1963

John Hewitt of Gothenburg fame was born in Aberdeen. Hewitt joined Aberdeen from Middlefield in 1979 and went on to become part of Pittodrie folklore by scoring the Dons' winning goal against Real Madrid in the 1983 European Cup Winners' Cup Final in Sweden. After leaving Aberdeen he played for Celtic and St Mirren before a brief spell coaching in Ireland.

SATURDAY 10TH FEBRUARY 1906

Rangers visited Pittodrie in the Scottish Cup. There were chaotic scenes at half-time as the Ibrox club lodged a protest over one of the Aberdeen players as they trailed 1-0. In those days the captain would hand over a written protest to the referee. Rangers protest was aimed at Paddy Boyle, the Aberdeen full-back who was alleged to have played for another club previously. The Rangers actions certainly wound up the home crowd and the second period was played in a very hostile atmosphere. A nasty game ended with Rangers winning 3-2.

SATURDAY 10TH FEBRUARY 1923

Peterhead were on the receiving end of a hammering, as Aberdeen chalked up a club record score against the-then Highland League side, crushing them 13-0 in Scottish Cup tie at Pittodrie. The tie was originally scheduled for Peterhead but their officials were keen to cash in on a big Pittodrie attendance. However, they had not consulted their players and there was open revolt within the Peterhead club. It was a disaster for them as wretched weather conditions kept the crowd down to a mere 3,241.

WEDNESDAY 10TH FEBRUARY 1965

Disaster for Aberdeen as they were sent crashing out of the Scottish Cup by lowly East Fife. It was the Dons' third successive exit against lower league opposition in the Cup and the 1-0 defeat was the final game in charge for manager Tommy Pearson. Aberdeen drew a blank in the first game played at Pittodrie and they were sent packing by a spirited East Fife in the replay at Bayview.

MONDAY 10TH FEBRUARY 1975

Following a 1-1 draw at Pittodrie, Aberdeen went to Ibrox for their third round Scottish Cup replay and shocked Rangers in a 2-1 win after extra time. Arthur Graham and Duncan Davidson scored the goals that took Aberdeen through to face Dundee United. This was also the first time that the Dons had beaten Rangers at Ibrox in the Scottish Cup. Davidson scored the winner after 112 minutes when Aberdeen sprang the Rangers offside trap before a stunned 52,000 crowd in Glasgow.

SATURDAY 11TH FEBRUARY 1961

Highland League side Deveronvale were hopeful of causing a real shock in the Scottish Cup when they came up against Aberdeen at Pittodrie. Included in the opposition were former Dons Reggie Morrison and Billy Smith. Their experience helped the part-time side to put pressure on the Dons but it was Charlie Cooke who made the difference as Aberdeen went on to win 4-2 before a 14,200 crowd.

WEDNESDAY 11TH FEBRUARY 1970

Martin Buchan was the youngest Aberdeen captain in the club's history as he guided the Dons through a difficult Scottish Cup tie against Clydebank. The game was originally postponed and on a rock hard surface Aberdeen struggled to defeat the part-timers. Aberdeen were forced to play in an unfamiliar blue striped kit that was borrowed at the last minute to save them clashing with the Bankies' red strip. After the 2-1 win, the Dons players were jeered as they left the field.

SATURDAY 12TH FEBRUARY 1921

Scotland welcomed Wales to Pittodrie for the second full international played in Aberdeen. A crowd of 20,824 paid £2,353 to see the Scots prevail in a 2-1 win with Andy Wilson scoring both goals. Pittodrie by that time had a new stand which was the first part of the current Main Stand at the stadium. Back then it was home to 1,000 spectators.

SATURDAY 13TH FEBRUARY 1954

Non-league Duns refused to switch this Dons Scottish Cup tie to Pittodrie and Aberdeen were faced with a nightmare trip to the Scottish Borders for what turned out to be an easy 8-0 win. The conditions were horrendous with the Duns pitch resembling a quagmire. Aberdeen had one of their smallest ever away supports that day as only six requests were made for tickets prior to the tie; a six-hour journey by car was the only way to reach the Borders outpost.

SATURDAY 14TH FEBRUARY 1931

Not many Dons players would experience what Lachlan McMillan went through in his 11-day career with Aberdeen. Signed from Hearts with a view to helping Aberdeen defeat Partick Thistle in a Scottish Cup replay, McMillan scored in the Dons' 3-0 triumph; a result that saw McMillan and new team-mate Benny Yorston carried shoulder high on their return to Aberdeen station. McMillan was also in the side that played Dundee at Dens Park in the next round. Unfortunately for him, he broke his leg after two minutes and his short Aberdeen career was over.

THURSDAY 14TH FEBRUARY 2008

Aberdeen qualified for the final 32 of the Uefa Cup and came up against old rivals Bayern Munich at Pittodrie. A spirited performance against the tournament favourites resulted in a 2-2 draw against the Germans, evoking fond memories of 1983 when the Dons knocked them out of the European Cup Winners' Cup. Goals from on-loan English youngsters Josh Walker and Sone Aluko gave Aberdeen a deserved first-half lead.

SATURDAY 15TH FEBRUARY 1964

Humiliation for Aberdeen as the Dons were sent crashing out of the Scottish Cup at home to Ayr United at Pittodrie. After reaching the third round, hopes were high that Aberdeen could make it all the way to the Hampden final. Ayr United were languishing at the bottom of the Second Division and were seen as mere fodder for the Reds. All seemed well when Billy Graham put the Dons ahead but late mistakes allowed the part-timers to embarrass their hosts and the majority of the 10,300 crowd.

SATURDAY 16TH FEBRUARY 1889

Orion were seen as the biggest and certainly most ambitious club that emerged in the Aberdeen area in the late 19th century. In what was the second Aberdeenshire Cup Final, Aberdeen defeated Orion 4-3 in a classic game that attracted a 3,000 crowd to the Chanonry. In the semi-finals, Aberdeen defeated Britannia 6-1, while Orion went through after a 6-2 win over Playfair.

SATURDAY 16TH FEBRUARY 1907

Charlie O'Hagan became the first Aberdeen player to represent his country when he was selected to play for Ireland against England. O'Hagan was seen as the first significant signing by Aberdeen and he went on to form a partnership with Willie Lennie on the left side of the Dons forward line.

SATURDAY 16TH FEBRUARY 1980

Former Aberdeen goalkeeper Ernie McGarr was back at Pittodrie with an Airdrie side as they faced the Dons in the Scottish Cup. He probably wished he had not bothered as Aberdeen humiliated the Broomfield side in an 8-0 drubbing that saw Steve Archibald enhance his growing reputation with four goals.

SATURDAY 17TH FEBRUARY 1912

West Lothian hopefuls Armadale visited Pittodrie on Scottish Cup duty after reaching the second round. Aberdeen were not used to being favourites but they progressed to the next round after a comfortable 3-0 win. The popular Jock Wyllie was among the scorer's before a crowd of 7,000 at Pittodrie.

SATURDAY 17TH FEBRUARY 1962

A classic Scottish Cup tie against Rangers attracted the biggest crowd of the season to Pittodrie when 41,139 filled the ground. This was the first all-ticket game at Pittodrie since the halcyon days of the title success in the 1950s. Aberdeen suffered a blow before the game as both Ken Brownlee and Willie Callaghan requested transfers. Three penalties were awarded in a pulsating encounter when Ogston saved Caldow's effort in the second half. The Dons deserved taking the tie to a replay after a 2-2 draw.

SATURDAY 18TH FEBRUARY 1995

It was a dark day for Aberdeen as they were humbled by Second Division Stenhousemuir in the Scottish Cup. The Reds went down 2-0 at Ochilview before a 3,452 crowd in what was regarded as the worst result for Aberdeen since their cup exit to East Fife in 1965.

WEDNESDAY 19TH FEBRUARY 1908

Aberdeen finally made it through to the last four of the Scottish Cup for the first time after a 3-1 win over Dundee. After a 0-0 draw at Pittodrie, the teams could not be separated in the Dens Park replay that finished 2-2. A crowd of 24,000 turned out at Hampden Park for the third game and it was Willie Lennie that rose from his sick bed to turn the game in the Abderdeen's favour with a stunning goal. It was reported back in Aberdeen that police had to be called to restore order outside the *Aberdeen Journal's* offices in Broad Street as news of the victory came through.

SATURDAY 20TH FEBRUARY 1954

Graham Leggat was brought into the Aberdeen first team as an emerging 19-year-old that was destined to become a Dons' all-time great. Aberdeen-born Leggat announced his arrival in style with three of the Reds five goals in a 5-3 win over Clyde. After a dreadful start to the season, Aberdeen were now in third place, level on points with second-placed Celtic.

SATURDAY 21st FEBRUARY 1953

Defending Cup holders Motherwell played their part in a classic Scottish Cup tie at Pittodrie. Aberdeen had just announced that Dave Shaw would be the new club trainer and he was in his usual place for the visit of Motherwell. The visitors held on and earned a replay in a thrilling 5-5 draw before 28,000 Aberdonians.

SATURDAY 21st FEBRUARY 1970

Despite a flu virus decimating the Aberdeen squad, a plea from the club to postpone their Scottish Cup quarter-final at Falkirk was dismissed by the SFA. Several players rose from their sick bed and answered the call, along with young Derek McKay who scored the winning goal that took Aberdeen through to the last four.

THURSDAY 21st FEBRUARY 2008

The Allianz Arena in Munich was the venue for the Dons' Uefa Cup last 32, second leg. Aberdeen had held Bayern to a 2-2 draw at Pittodrie but were well beaten 5-1 in the return. The 66,000 attendance created a new record crowd for Aberdeen in European competition.

SATURDAY 22nd FEBRUARY 1908

Tom Murray became the first Aberdeen player to score three goals in a Scottish Cup match for the Dons when Aberdeen beat Queen's Park 3-1 at Pittodrie. Middlesbrough-born Murray made an immediate impact after signing in May 1907 by scoring a new club record of 19 goals in his first season. Rangers signed Murray in 1908 but he returned to Pittodrie after a year with the Ibrox club.

SATURDAY 22nd FEBRUARY 1964

Aberdeen regained their previous good record to take both points in a hard-fought game against Falkirk at Brockville. Ernie Winchester added to his growing reputation with another two goals in the Dons' 3-2 win over the 'Bairns'. After Maxwell pulled a goal back for the home side on 74 minutes, the Reds were up against it as Falkirk managed to muster 15 corner kicks in the final ten minutes.

WEDNESDAY 22ND FEBRUARY 1978

Stuart Kennedy made his Scotland debut against Bulgaria at Hampden Park in the Scots 2-1 win. Kennedy was signed by Ally Macleod for £25,000 in July 1976 and the former Falkirk full-back went on to become a firm favourite at Pittodrie. Once described by Alex Ferguson as the best professional he had ever worked with, an injury sustained against Waterschei, in the 1983 European Cup Winners' Cup tie in Belgium, effectively ended his career.

SATURDAY 23RD FEBRUARY 1952

Division 'B' hopefuls Dundee United pushed Aberdeen all the way in the Scottish Cup at Tannadice. The Reds had gone ahead through Archie Baird after Harry Yorston had cancelled out Cruickshank's opener. After Dunsmore had missed a penalty, McKay earned the Dundee side a replay after the 2-2 draw attracted a then club record attendance of 26,000.

SATURDAY 24TH FEBRUARY 1906

Stewart Davidson, signed from Shamrock Rovers in 1905, made his first team debut for Aberdeen against Motherwell at Pittodrie. Davidson enjoyed two spells with the Dons, split by the war and a transfer to Middlesbrough in April 1913. Davidson returned to Pittodrie in May 1923 and, in all, played 149 matches for the club and was also capped for Scotland.

SATURDAY 24TH FEBRUARY 1912

There was a new attendance record for Pittodrie as 22,000 filled the ground for the visit of Celtic in the Scottish Cup. After losing to the Parkhead club in 1908, 1910 and in 1911, Aberdeen were determined change matters. A classic cup tie finished 2-2 with top scorer Davie Main on target for Aberdeen. Celtic won the replay 2-0.

SATURDAY 24TH FEBRUARY 1923

After three matches, Aberdeen 'A' eventually defeated a determined Buckie Thistle to reach the final of the Aberdeenshire Cup. The young Dons made it through after 2-2 and 0-0 draws. The last meeting ended with Aberdeen taking the tie back to Pittodrie and winning 3-2. The Aberdeen reserve side went on to defeat Fraserburgh 4-0 in the final.

SATURDAY 25TH FEBRUARY 1911

WD Nicol or 'thunderbolt' as he was better known, became the first Aberdeen player to score five goals in a Scottish Cup match when the Dons beat Forfar Athletic at Pittodrie in a third round tie. Nicol only played 11 games for Aberdeen, scoring seven goals, in a short, but memorable, career.

SUNDAY 25TH FEBRUARY 1934

Paddy Moore was a prolific scorer for Aberdeen in his short spell with the Dons. Moore was an Ireland international and he scored four goals for his country in a World Cup tie in Dublin against Belgium. It was all the more remarkable as Moore's Irish side were at one point trailing by 4-0 in the game!

SATURDAY 26TH FEBRUARY 2000

In a troubled first season for Aberdeen boss Ebbe Skovdahl, the Dons recorded their best victory of the season in a 4-0 win over Hibernian to offer the Dane some respite. Russell Anderson was among the goals with 12,655 in attendance at Pittodrie. Top scorer Arild Stavrum scored two as the Dons looked to get away from the bottom of the league. This was only the Reds' sixth win of the season and a third victory in a row.

SATURDAY 27TH FEBRUARY 1954

Aberdeen's hold over Hibernian in cup football continued with a 3-1 win over the Easter Road side in the third round of the Scottish Cup. Jackie Hather was expected to miss the game through injury but was a surprise inclusion in the starting XI. Inside seven minutes he had put Aberdeen two goals ahead to stun the 47,700 crowd.

WEDNESDAY 27TH FEBRUARY 1974

As the country was grinding to a halt during the three-day working week and the enforced power cuts, Scotland under-23s defeated Wales 3-0 at Pittodrie. The attendance was around the 15,000 mark which was due to the afternoon kick-off as no floodlighting was permitted.

FRIDAY 28TH FEBRUARY 1965

Eddie Turnbull was unveiled as new Aberdeen manager at a Pittodrie press conference. Turnbull was part of the famed 'Famous Five' with Hibernian in the 1950s and had been the Dons' choice to lead the club into a new era after cutting his coaching teeth at Queen's Park. Within weeks of his appointment, Turnbull began his revolution by releasing an incredible 17 players on free transfers.

SATURDAY 29TH FEBRUARY 1936

The shock of this, or any other season, as Aberdeen inexplicably lose at home to Arbroath. Aberdeen had been challenging at the top of the table all campaign and were in the midst of breaking all their own club records in the league. They went into the game with only one defeat in their previous 20 matches. Following the 2-1 loss to their Angus neighbours, the Dons would not lose another game that season; dropping only one point from their final seven matches. It was not enough to take the title as the black & golds finished five points behind champions Celtic.

SATURDAY 29TH FEBRUARY 1992

Aberdeen were struggling to reach the heights of previous years as the pressure grew on manager Alex Smith. The Dons boss was given some respite after a 2-0 win over St Mirren in Paisley. Paul Mason, and a rare goal from young Gary Smith, gave Aberdeen both points before a poor 3,853 crowd. St Mirren were cut adrift at the bottom of the league along with relegation certainties Dunfermline Athletic.

ABERDEEN FC
On This Day

MARCH

SATURDAY 1st MARCH 1947

After finishing as League Cup group winners, the Dons came up against Dundee in the quarter-final. Played over two legs, Aberdeen seized a vital first leg lead after a 1-0 win at Dens Park. On an icy pitch, former Dons Bobby Ancell and Jock Pattillo could not prevent a Willie Millar goal in 51 minutes handing Aberdeen control of the tie. The Reds went on to win the tie 4-2 on aggregate.

SATURDAY 1st MARCH 1969

Despite a poor run of results in the league, Aberdeen did little wrong in the Cup. Against Kilmarnock at Pittodrie the quarter-final clash ended in a 0-0 stalemate and the nearest the Dons came to scoring was when McLaughlan turned a Davie Johnston shot against the post. The 24,000 crowd were left frustrated by Kilmarnock's defensive tactics. Three days later the Dons played their fourth cup tie in nine days, winning a 3-0 replay win at Rugby Park.

SATURDAY 2nd MARCH 1907

Pittodrie was the scene of chaos after undefeated Celtic escaped with a 2-2 draw. Several refereeing decisions did not go the home side's way as they had the ball in the net on no less than four occasions, but were denied by some baffling decisions. Referee Jackson came in for a torrent of abuse from the Pittodrie support, and when the final whistle blew the pitch was invaded by angry supporters. Police eventually restored calm as the referee made his way to the relative safety of the changing rooms.

WEDNESDAY 2nd MARCH 1977

Disaster for Aberdeen. The 18,375 crowd were shocked to see a mistake by Willie Miller which allowed Dundee to progress in this Scottish Cup replay. The visitors were inspired by a young Gordon Strachan who did not look out of place against far more experienced opponents. Malicious talk of a betting scam after the game was dismissed after it emerged that it was a hoax call to the local press.

WEDNESDAY 2ND MARCH 1983

The Olympic Stadium in Munich was the venue for the Dons biggest European challenge in their history. Reaching the last eight of the European Cup Winners' Cup, Aberdeen were in new territory. The 35,000 crowd expected a comfortable win for Bayern over their Scottish opponents; what they saw was a technically sound performance for an Aberdeen side that more than held their own against some of the best players in world football. The 0-0 draw meant that Aberdeen had an outstanding opportunity to reach the semi-finals.

WEDNESDAY 3RD MARCH 1954

Teddy Scott signed for Aberdeen to begin a remarkable association with the club. Teddy was part of the successful Sunnybank side that became the first Aberdeen club to win the Junior Cup. He was called up to Aberdeen that summer. Although he never established himself in the first team it was as a trainer in the 1970s that Teddy became part of the surroundings at the club. In 2003 Teddy retired after enjoying a superb testimonial against Manchester United at Pittodrie in 1999.

SATURDAY 4TH MARCH 1978

A win at Ibrox was a must for Aberdeen as they continued their pursuit of Rangers at the league summit. The Dons duly delivered a second successive crushing blow with a 3-0 win before a 40,000 crowd. Steve Archibald, the Dons new signing from Clyde, scored twice as the Ibrox stands cleared long before the final whistle. This was Rangers' first defeat since their 4-0 loss at Aberdeen in December.

SATURDAY 5TH MARCH 1904

The final of the Aberdeenshire Cup took place at Pittodrie and for the last time it was the Aberdeen first team that competed. Goals from Mackie, Sangster and MacAulay gave Aberdeen a 3-0 win over Bon Accord before a 2,000 crowd. With the club moving into the Scottish League, it would be the reserve side that would compete in the Aberdeenshire Cup in future.

WEDNESDAY 5TH MARCH 1986

The last four of the European Champions Cup beckoned for Aberdeen as they came up against Swedish side Gothenburg at Pittodrie. Willie Miller marked his 50th European appearance for the Reds by scoring the opening goal. Despite John Hewitt putting Aberdeen ahead for the second time in 79 minutes, a late lapse allowed Johnny Ekstrom to score a crucial leveller in the last minute. Aberdeen were set for an emotional return to the Ullevi Stadium in the return leg…

SATURDAY 6TH MARCH 1911

Donald Colman became the oldest Aberdeen player to be capped when he played for Scotland against Wales at Ninian Park at the age of 33. Colman actually changed his surname to disguise the fact that he played football from his father some years previously. Colman went on to become Aberdeen trainer.

SUNDAY 6TH MARCH 1949

Martin Buchan, who remains the youngest ever captain to win the Scottish Cup, was born in Aberdeen. After joining the Dons in 1965, Buchan went on to become one of the finest defenders ever produced by Aberdeen and in 1970, as a young 21-year-old, he was captain of the Dons side that defeated Celtic at Hampden Park in the Scottish Cup Final. Buchan went on to win the FA Cup with Manchester United after his switch to Old Trafford in 1972 and went on to play on 34 occasions for Scotland.

SATURDAY 7TH MARCH 1908

Willie Lennie became the first Aberdeen player to play for Scotland when he turned out against Wales at Dens Park in Dundee. Lennie scored the winning goal in a 2-1 win for the Scots. The Aberdeen winger was a firm favourite at Pittodrie and had been signed from Fulham in 1905. He went on to make 251 appearances for Aberdeen before joining Falkirk for £30 in 1913.

WEDNESDAY 7TH MARCH 1984

Aberdeen suffered their first defeat in 28 matches when they went down 2-0 to Ujpest Dosza in the Megyeri Stadium in Budapest. Their European Cup Winners' Cup quarter-final first leg was about as bad as it gets as the Dons dominated the game but missed several chances, with Mark McGhee's miss from two yards in the 'unbelievable' category.

SATURDAY 8TH MARCH 1969

After some memorable Cup exploits, the Dons first league game for five weeks ended in an incredible defeat at Arbroath. The Gayfield side were rooted to the bottom of the league but summoned up enough fight to give the Dons the worst of preparations for their Scottish Cup meeting with Rangers. Ernie McGarr had good cause to complain as he was unceremoniously barged over the line by Sellars to give Arbroath an unlikely win before a 4,700 crowd.

SATURDAY 9TH MARCH 1935

Celtic's cup hoodoo over Aberdeen was finally broken when Aberdeen defeated the Glasgow side 3-1 at Pittodrie. It was a first-ever win over Celtic in the Cup and Matt Armstrong scored twice before a huge 40,105 – and record – Pittodrie crowd.

SATURDAY 11TH MARCH 1882

Coupar Angus provided the first-ever opposition for the original Aberdeen FC in 1882. The fledgling Aberdeen club travelled south and were beaten 4-0 against a more experienced side. It was reported that the teams enjoyed a 'scrumptious repast' in the Royal Hotel after the game.

WEDNESDAY 11TH MARCH 1964

The date for the Dons' biggest home crowd of the season, as 22,000 turned out for the visit of champions Rangers. This one was no place for the faint of heart as Aberdeen set about upsetting their visitors from the start. Willie Henderson was taken off with an ankle injury while Jim Forrest was also a virtual passenger after taking a heavy knock early in the game. Ernie Winchester scored his almost obligatory goal before Jim Baxter levelled from a 50th minute penalty.

WEDNESDAY 12TH MARCH 1975

Billy Williamson was the Aberdeen hero as he scored all three goals in a 3-2 win over Celtic at Pittodrie. Earlier in the day, the Reds captain shocked the club by announcing that he was leaving at the end of the season to join the police. Williamson completed the Dons win by taking a 78th minute penalty that beat Latchford to give Aberdeen their first home win over Celtic for nine years.

SUNDAY 12TH MARCH 2000

Despite some woeful form in the league, Aberdeen could do little wrong in the Cup competitions. Against Dundee United at Tannadice in the quarter-final of the Scottish Cup, a solitary goal from Eoin Jess was enough to put Aberdeen through to the last four before a poor 6,738 crowd.

SATURDAY 13TH MARCH 1954

Pittodrie was full for a Scottish Cup tie against league leaders Hearts that attracted a club record attendance of 45,061. Joe O'Neil made the breakthrough with a superb volley from the edge of the box just before the interval. Further goals from Leggat and Hamilton helped Aberdeen ease their way through to the last four.

SATURDAY 13TH MARCH 1982

Jim Leighton was the Aberdeen hero as he saved a Jim Bett penalty with the Dons 1-0 ahead against Rangers at Ibrox. It paved the way for a 3-1 win that kept Aberdeen in the race for the title. Steve Cowan and Neale Cooper had the Dons two goals ahead before the break.

SATURDAY 14TH MARCH 1970

Derek McKay continued his Cup heroics by scoring the goal that took Aberdeen through to the final at Hampden Park when the Dons defeated Kilmarnock 1-0 at Muirton Park in Perth. The bulk of the 28,000 crowd were from Aberdeen as trouble flared. McKay had kept his place in the side and his goal in 21 minutes was enough to put the Reds through to meet Celtic.

DEREK McKAY SCORES THE WINNER IN THE SCOTTISH CUP SEMI-FINAL IN 1970

WEDNESDAY 14th MARCH 1979

After a 1-1 draw at Pittodrie, the Dons went to Celtic and won their Scottish Cup replay 2-1 in what was a hostile atmosphere at the Glasgow ground. Trouble broke out between both sets of players at the final whistle as the Aberdeen players celebrated. Reds goalkeeper Bobby Clark was punched as the flare up continued outside the dressing rooms.

SATURDAY 15th MARCH 2008

The game that almost never happened as crisis club Gretna managed to scramble a team together to play Aberdeen at Pittodrie. The tiny Borders club may have been out of their depth in the SPL but they were faced with going out of business after financial backing was withdrawn. As the administrators moved in, Aberdeen showed little sympathy and cruised to a 3-0 win as doubts over Gretna's ability to see out the season remained.

WEDNESDAY 16th MARCH 1983

It was the greatest night ever at Pittodrie as Aberdeen defeated Bayern Munich to progress to the last four of the European Cup Winners' Cup. After a 0-0 draw in Germany, Aberdeen looked out after Bayern took a 2-1 lead in the second period. However, two goals in a minute from Alex McLeish, then John Hewitt, had changed things and it was Aberdeen that prevailed in a sensational win over the tournament favourites. It was the last European appearance for Munich captain Paul Breitner.

WEDNESDAY 17th MARCH 1954

Aberdeen had gained momentum in the Scottish Cup and were also battling to stay in contention in the league. With Archie Glen and Paddy Buckley playing for Scotland against Ireland in Dublin, Aberdeen lost vital ground with a disappointing 1-0 defeat at home to Falkirk. The Dons dominated and hit the woodwork on four occasions. Worse still for Aberdeen was the bad head injury to Joe O'Neil; his fractured skull was giving cause for concern, and he was rushed to Aberdeen Infirmary.

SATURDAY 18TH MARCH 1905

Aberdeen reserves continued the clubs' impressive record in the Aberdeenshire Cup by winning the trophy after the first-team had been withdrawn from competing. After defeating Bon Accord 3-1 in the semi-final, the reserves beat Harp 3-2 at Pittodrie.

SATURDAY 18TH MARCH 1939

The famous black and gold strip that Aberdeen had worn since 1904 was discarded for new red shirts and white shorts for the visit of Queen's Park. The Reds would retain red as their colours; the only top-flight club in Scotland to do so.

WEDNESDAY 18TH MARCH 1953

A huge 47,500 crowd turned out for the Dons' quarter-final Scottish Cup clash against Hibernian at Easter Road. Over 7,000 Aberdeen fans saw their side take Hibs back to Pittodrie for a replay with a 1-1 draw. A double from George Hamilton in the replay sent the Dons marching on to the semi-finals before 42,000 at Pittodrie.

WEDNESDAY 19TH MARCH 1986

Gothenburg knocked the Dons out of the European Cup as Aberdeen reached the last eight for the first time. After a 2-2 draw at Pittodrie, the Dons 0-0 result in the Ullevi Stadium was not enough to take Aberdeen through to the last four.

SUNDAY 19TH MARCH 2000

The Dons lost out to Celtic in the final of the League Cup at Hampden. Thomas Solberg was sent off in a game that Aberdeen rarely threatened. With Derek Whyte suspended the Dons were fortunate not to go down by more than the 2-0 defeat in what was a first Hampden final for new manager Ebbe Skovdahl.

TUESDAY 20TH MARCH 1962

A timely win for Aberdeen as the 5-3 success at Third Lanark guaranteed safety. The Dons rang the changes after poor results against Hibernian and Dunfermline Athletic at Pittodrie. In came Ally Shewan, Willie Allan, Charlie Cooke and Willie Callaghan with Ken Brownlee scoring twice to keep the Dons ahead against the Cathkin Park side.

SATURDAY 21st MARCH 1908

Aberdeen reached the last four of the Scottish Cup for the first time before going down 1-0 to Celtic at Pittodrie. The game attracted 19,294 fans that paid through the gate. Ladies were given free admission. There were chaotic scenes at the end of the game as the visiting players were pelted with stones after their physical approach to the game was not best received by the home support. Charlie O'Hagan in particular was targeted and it was counted that he was fouled six times in five minutes. It was reported that 43 tram cars took more than 7,500 supporters to Pittodrie before the game.

SATURDAY 21st MARCH 1970

Arthur Graham made his first team debut for Aberdeen against Dunfermline Athletic at Pittodrie. Graham had recently been signed from Cambuslang and was spotted by legendary Aberdeen scout Bobby Calder. 'Bumper', as he became known, kept his place in the side and he went on to help Aberdeen win the Scottish Cup weeks later in a 3-1 win over Celtic.

WEDNESDAY 21st MARCH 1973

Following a brave 0-0 draw against Celtic in the Scottish Cup quarter-final at Parkhead, Aberdeen were eventually beaten by a late Billy McNeill goal in the replay before a 33,465 Pittodrie crowd. There was plenty of controversy as Jim Hermiston was harshly adjudged to have impeded Jimmy Johnstone for the free-kick that gave Celtic the winning goal on 86 minutes.

WEDNESDAY 21st MARCH 1984

Mark McGhee was the Aberdeen hero as the Dons held on to hopes of retaining the European Cup Winners' Cup with an extra time win over Hungarian side Ujpest Dozsa in a dramatic quarter-final second leg at Pittodrie. Trailing 2-0 from the first game in Budapest, McGhee scored all three Aberdeen goals, his second coming five minutes from time to take the tie into extra time.

SATURDAY 22ND MARCH 1902

Aberdeen won the Dewar Shield final after a 1-0 win over Dundee Wanderers in Dundee. The result gave the Aberdeen club fresh impetus to launch another application to join the Scottish League. The game attracted a crowd of 4,000, and it was reported that around 500 supporters from the north had followed Aberdeen to the final.

SATURDAY 22ND MARCH 1924

Aberdeen were held in a 0-0 draw in their bid to reach their first Scottish Cup Final against Hibernian at Dens Park in Dundee. The 20,000 crowd saw Johnny Miller go close for the Dons but it was goalkeeper Harry Blackwell who kept his side in it with some great saves in the second period. While the first team were in Dundee, the Aberdeen reserves led the way with a 6-0 win over Keith to win the Aberdeenshire Cup. The reserves had previously hammered Aberdeen University 6-0 and Peterhead 7-0 on the way to the Pittodrie final.

SATURDAY 22ND MARCH 1947

Hearts proud record in the League Cup was crushed by Aberdeen as the Dons hit the Tynecastle side for six in the semi-final clash at Easter Road. George Hamilton scored three in a second half that Aberdeen dominated after falling behind in the first period. The Dons played in an unfamiliar blue shirt with white sleeves before a 36,200 crowd.

WEDNESDAY 22ND MARCH 1967

The biggest ever midweek attendance at Pittodrie – an estimated 44,000 crowd – filled the ground with some spectators risking life and limb by climbing up on to the floodlight stanchions and the roof at the Beach End part of the ground. The reason for the excitement was a quarter-final Scottish Cup replay against Hibernian. Tensions were high after the first game ended in a 1-1 draw. Eddie Turnbull promised his old side a 'warm' welcome and the Dons demolished the Easter Road side 3-0 to make it through to the last four.

MONDAY 23RD MARCH 1964

While it is widely accepted that the biggest change in the Scottish football set up was the inception of the Premier League in 1975, in 1964 the 37 member clubs voted on a proposed structure of 12, 12 and 13 to replace the existing 18-team First Division and 19 in the second tier. At that time attendances all over the country had plummeted and there was real concern among member clubs. The proposals, however, were seen as too radical and the motion was not approved.

SATURDAY 24TH MARCH 1888

The first-ever Aberdeenshire Cup Final took place at the Chanonry in Old Aberdeen. Aberdeen defeated Aberdeen Rangers 7-1 to lift the trophy for the first time. An estimated crowd of 1,000 filled every vantage point in the tight confines of the old ground. Aberdeen had gone the entire 1887/88 season undefeated.

TUESDAY 24TH MARCH 1992

One of the most memorable matches ever at Pittodrie as Scotland under-21s defeated Germany in the quarter-final of their European Championship match. After a 1-1 draw in Germany in the first leg, the Scots looked out when they went 3-1 down in the return after an hour of play. A capacity 22,500 crowd urged the Scots on as they clawed their way back into the game and when Alex Rae scored the winner with two minutes left, calmly lobbing Stefan Klos from the edge of the area, the huge crowd went wild with delight.

WEDNESDAY 25TH MARCH 1970

Celtic loaded their dressing room with champagne before their game against Aberdeen at Parkhead, much to the dismay of manager Eddie Turnbull. Needing two points to clinch the title, Celtic were confident ahead of the visit from the Dons. Young winger Arthur Graham was thrown into the Parkhead cauldron as Aberdeen set about keeping the champers on ice in a 2-1 win.

ABERDEEN SHOW OFF THE SILVERWARE, CIRCA 1900

SATURDAY 25TH MARCH 1972

Bizarre refereeing from Dundee whistler Bob Valentine contrived to anger the home support despite Aberdeen easing to a 4-1 win over Motherwell. Valentine refused two blatant penalty claims from the Dons before sending Jim Hermiston off for a minor infringement. When all the controversy had calmed down late goals from Harper and Robb failed to prevent Valentine getting a roasting from the 10,000 crowd at full-time.

SUNDAY 26TH MARCH 1905

Scotland international Andy Love was born in Renfrew. Love joined Aberdeen in 1925 and went on to become a first team regular two years later as he replaced Alec Reid in the first team. Love went on to play for Scotland and he made 237 appearances – scoring 83 goals – for Aberdeen. Love was one of several players who never received a cap from his country as his appearances came against foreign opposition. That rule was changed by the SFA in 2005 to make sure that all of the players were recognised.

MONDAY 26TH MARCH 1979

Joe Harper led the way with three goals as Aberdeen racked up a Premier League record score in an 8-0 win over Motherwell at Pittodrie. It was a dark day for Ally MacLeod who was Motherwell manager at the time. MacLeod had spent happier days during his time in charge at Aberdeen. The game proved to be the ideal preparation for the Reds as they looked forward to the League Cup Final against Rangers.

WEDNESDAY 26TH MARCH 1980

Alex McLeish made his first appearance for Scotland in a 4-1 win over Portugal at Hampden in a European Championship tie. McLeish went on to become the Dons most capped player with 77 appearances for his country. Steve Archibald was also a Scotland debutant that evening; the young Aberdeen striker came on as a substitute and scored the Scots third goal in 68 minutes.

WEDNESDAY 26TH MARCH 2003

Old European rivals SV Hamburg visited Pittodrie to help celebrate the Dons Centenary. Hamburg had been opponents in four previous matches and the Dons went down 3-2 against the Bundesliga side before a poor crowd of less than 4,000, which was a disappointment to the club and the Centenary organisers.

SATURDAY 27TH MARCH 1909

As Aberdeen were going down 3-1 at Ibrox in the league, it was all happening at Pittodrie. The Aberdeen 'A' team was involved in a dramatic game against their Dundee counterparts as their Dewar Shield meeting ended in a 2-2 draw. Despite the new extra time law that was in place the Dundee players refused to continue and walked off the field! Aberdeen went on to claim the tie, which was upheld.

SATURDAY 27TH MARCH 1915

There were ugly scenes at Ibrox as several Aberdeen players were involved in a fracas with Rangers supporters after the teams had fought out a 1-1 draw. The result ended Rangers faint hopes of taking the league title. Owing to the events of the war in Europe, Aberdeen did not take the matter further.

SATURDAY 27TH MARCH 1926

A first-ever league double over Rangers for Aberdeen after a 1-0 win over their Ibrox rivals in Glasgow. Alec Reid scored the winning goal after the Dons had defeated Rangers 3-1 at Pittodrie earlier in the season. Aberdeen failed to build on their win by losing 4-1 to Celtic a week later.

SATURDAY 27TH MARCH 1937

Aberdeen finished their home matches in the league with an impressive 4-0 win over Hearts. Billy Strauss and Matt Armstrong scored two goals each before a 16,000 crowd and remained undefeated at home in all matches during the entire 1936/37 season. The Dons still had four games left to play; all away from home. Aberdeen went on to finish as runners-up in the championship, two points ahead of third-placed Celtic.

WEDNESDAY 28TH MARCH 1990

Stewart McKimmie had the distinction of scoring the winning goal against the World Cup winners. His superb half-volley in the 32nd minute helped Scotland to a shock 1-0 win over Argentina before a 51,537 attendance at Hampden Park. Alex McLeish and Jim Bett were the other Aberdeen players in the side that night.

SATURDAY 29TH MARCH 1902

Aberdeen's Northern League hopes were dealt a blow as they went down 2-1 to title challengers Dundee Wanderers at Clepington Park in Dundee. Back in Aberdeen, Orion and Victoria United shared the honours in a 2-2 draw, while the young Orion reserve side were hammered 10-2 by Peterhead in a friendly.

TUESDAY 29TH MARCH 1966

Aberdeen went down 2-1 to Rangers in their Scottish Cup semi-final replay at Hampden. The Reds were looking to reach their first final since 1959 and after a 0-0 draw in the first game, the Dons were finally beaten when a McLean shot eluded Bobby Clark on 80 minutes. Earlier, Harry Melrose brought Aberdeen level after Jim Forrest had opened the scoring for Rangers. The Dons never looked convincing enough to win the tie before a 40,850 crowd.

SATURDAY 30TH MARCH 1963

One of the darkest days in the club's history as the Dons were humbled in the Scottish Cup. Despite beating Raith Rovers 10-0 in the league at Pittodrie several weeks earlier, Aberdeen went down 2-1 at Kirkcaldy in a quarter-final tie. Raith had not won a home game all season and were destined to finish bottom with only nine points from 34 matches. It was a late goal by Gilfilan that proved to be the winner that piled the pressure on Aberdeen to arrest the alarming decline. Some weeks later Aberdeen defeated Raith 4-0 in the league at the same venue.

SATURDAY 31ST MARCH 1979

Disappointment for Aberdeen as they went down 2-1 to Rangers in the League Cup Final. The match was shrouded in controversy as Doug Rougvie was sent off after a clash with Rangers' Derek Johnstone. It was Alex Ferguson's first final in charge of Aberdeen.

ABERDEEN FC
On This Day

APRIL

SATURDAY 1st APRIL 1967

The Dons reached their first Scottish Cup Final since 1959 with a narrow 1-0 win over Dundee United at Dens Park. Despite the game being played in Dundee, it was Aberdeen supporters that made up the bulk of the near 35,000 attendance. The game was settled after a piece of Jimmy Smith magic. Smith had forced a corner after a wild clearance from Briggs. United keeper Davie failed to hold the cross and as Smith flicked the ball across goal, Tommy Millar turned it into his own net.

TUESDAY 1st APRIL 1980

One of the Dons' matches in hand, as they chased Celtic for the title, came against Kilmarnock at Rugby Park. The Reds had managed to carve open the home side at will, and their 4-0 win was an ominous sign for Celtic as Aberdeen were finding form at the right time of the season. Pick of the goals was a surging run from Stuart Kennedy in 78 minutes as he finished off a clinical Aberdeen break.

SATURDAY 1st APRIL 1989

With the league race reaching the closing stages, Aberdeen defeated Dundee United 1-0 at Pittodrie to keep on the tails of leaders Rangers. Charlie Nicholas scored the all-important goal as the win ended any faint United hopes of catching the top two. This was the Dons sixth league win in succession, closing the gap at the top to three points.

SATURDAY 2nd APRIL 1904

Despite two goals from Charlie Mackie, Aberdeen were hammered 8-3 by Falkirk in the Dewar Shield at Brockville. It was the new club's worst defeat in their short existence. With Falkirk not even being in the First Division, it was clear that Aberdeen had some way to go to be able to compete at the highest level. Back at Pittodrie, the reserves drew 2-2 with Peterhead in a friendly before a 1,500 crowd.

SATURDAY 2ND APRIL 1955

The day that many believed that Aberdeen clinched their first league title. Rangers were swept aside at Pittodrie in a 4-0 win before a 32,000 crowd. Aberdeen were without Fred Martin who was on duty for Scotland against England at Wembley, but a sensational three goals from Paddy Buckley ensured that the Dons were almost there in the race for the league flag. It was reported that 'hundreds of bunnets were thrown to the air in joy' after Buckley scored the Dons' third goal. Rangers were at full strength with no players selected for international duty.

SATURDAY 3RD APRIL 1948

A record 43,800 crowd filled Pittodrie for the visit of Rangers in what was the Dons last home game of the season. Aberdeen were free from any relegation worries while the visitors were pursuing Hibernian at the summit. The stadium gates were locked before the start and Aberdeen were unlucky not finish their season with a win as Rangers held out for a 1-1 draw.

SATURDAY 3RD APRIL 1993

Scott Booth was the Aberdeen hero as his goal put his side through to the Scottish Cup Final after a 1-0 win over Hibernian at Tynecastle. The Dons had beaten Hamilton, Dundee United and Clydebank but were without the services of Eoin Jess who had broken his leg in an earlier round.

MONDAY 4TH APRIL 1966

A low-key debut for Jimmy 'Jinky' Smith, who would go on to become a cult figure at Pittodrie. Smith was brought into the side to replace Danish signing Jorg Ravn as Aberdeen went on to pile more relegation misery on Morton with a 5-3 win before a poor 3,500 Pittodrie crowd. The Reds were recovering from losing out in a Scottish Cup semi-final replay against Rangers, but allowed Morton back into the game before late goals from Billy Little and Jimmy Wilson restored the Dons two-goal cushion.

SATURDAY 5TH APRIL 1947

Disaster for Aberdeen as they lost the League Cup Final to Rangers at Hampden Park. This was the first official cup final since the war and Aberdeen prepared for the game by spending several days in their base at Largs. The 4-0 defeat was hardly a fair reflection as Aberdeen captain Frank Dunlop won the toss and decided to play against gale-force winds and driving rain. It was a decision that was to cost the Dons as they went in at the break three goals down. Despite this, the Reds should have got back into the game in a second period that saw two valid penalty claims brushed aside.

SATURDAY 5TH APRIL 1980

Aberdeen simply had to win as Celtic closed in on the league title. Mark McGhee rounded Latchford to set up Drew Jarvie to open the scoring while Doyle levelled for the home side in 23 minutes. Ian Scanlon then had his shot blocked before McGhee made sure from the rebound. At 2-1 for Aberdeen the late drama centred round Bobby Clark's goal as Celtic were awarded a controversial penalty. Clark dived to save from Lennox in what must have been sweet revenge for the Aberdeen veteran after Lennox's colourful history.

SATURDAY 6TH APRIL 1929

Hugh McLaren certainly made his mark for both Aberdeen and Kilmarnock in 1929. The Dons centre-half had been part of the successful Aberdeen side of that era. However, by a strange twist of fate he would go on to help Kilmarnock to cup glory. The Rugby Park side were seeking a temporary replacement for the injured Dunlop and an agreement was reached with Aberdeen that McLaren would be loaned to them for Cup matches only. Kilmarnock defeated Rangers at Hampden Park that day to lift the Scottish Cup. Seven days later, McLaren was back in the Aberdeen reserve side playing St Johnstone!

WEDNESDAY 6TH APRIL 1983

With a worldwide television audience watching, Aberdeen set about destroying Belgian side Waterschei in the first leg of the European Cup Winners' Cup semi-final at Pittodrie. Two goals in the opening four minutes set the tone for a game that Aberdeen showed all of their power and passion. The eventual 5-1 win had the Red Army hunting for their passports for Sweden...

WEDNESDAY 7TH APRIL 1982

Peter Weir emerged as the Aberdeen hero as he scored the goal that put Aberdeen through to the Scottish Cup Final after a thrilling 3-2 replay win against St Mirren. Dens Park was the venue for a game that attracted a 15,670 crowd. Neil Simpson forced an early error from Thomson while the heavy conditions played a part. After Thomson had let Weir's tame effort slip through his legs, it was the Dons that were rejoicing in the rain.

SATURDAY 8TH APRIL 1967

The Dons moved into third place as the race for European football gathered momentum after they had beaten Falkirk 6-1. Harry Melrose was back as Aberdeen captain on his return to the side. With Hibernian, Clyde and Kilmarnock all chasing the Reds for a place in Europe, the Dons first win in five games was a welcome boost for the 7,000 Pittodrie crowd.

SATURDAY 9TH APRIL 1921

Two Aberdeen-born players were capped for Scotland for the first time in the same international, against England at Hampden. Former Dons George Brewster and Stewart Davidson both took their bow before an 85,000 crowd. Davidson was with Middlesbrough at that time while Brewster was with Everton.

SATURDAY 9TH APRIL 1955

Clyde's Shawfield Stadium was where Aberdeen won the League championship for the first time. A 1-0 win ensured that the Dons could not be caught by Celtic with two games left. Archie Glen scored from a penalty after George Hamilton's net-bound header was punched by a Clyde defender. It was Hamilton's last match for the club.

SATURDAY 10TH APRIL 1954

A first-ever Scottish Cup win over Rangers was completed in style as a rampant Aberdeen inflicted a 6-0 defeat on their great rivals which remains the worst Scottish Cup defeat in the Glasgow club's history. Joe O'Neil was the Aberdeen hero with three goals only days after he received a fractured skull in a game against Falkirk. O'Neil went against medical advice to take his place in the side against the club that had snubbed him as a youngster after they learned what school he attended. The Aberdeen support, in the estimated crowd of 111,000, were ecstatic as Rangers famed 'Iron Curtain' defence was ripped apart.

SATURDAY 11TH APRIL 1970

Derek McKay and Joe Harper scored the goals that won the Scottish Cup for the second time in the Dons' history after a sensational 3-1 win over Celtic at Hampden. The Reds were rank outsiders against a side that was in the midst of embarrassing Don Revie's Leeds United in the European Cup. However, Aberdeen were confident enough to hit Celtic with lightning pace and it was a dream day for Derek 'Cup-tie' McKay whose only real contribution for Aberdeen was winning goals in the quarter-final, semi-final and Final that season. Joe Harper opened the scoring with a penalty, the Dons' 500th goal in the Scottish Cup.

WEDNESDAY 11TH APRIL 1984

In front of their biggest attendance in a European tie, the Dons went down 1-0 to Porto before a passionate 65,000 crowd in the first leg of their European Cup Winners' Cup semi-final in Portugal. A Gomes header after 14 minutes was enough to give the home side the advantage. It took a superb defensive display from Aberdeen in the second half to keep Porto out as passions ran high on and off the field. In the other semi-final Manchester United were playing Juventus.

SATURDAY 12TH APRIL 1947

After six previous failed attempts to reach the Scottish Cup Final, Aberdeen finally laid their Cup hoodoo to rest after a 2-0 win over Arbroath at Dens Park. 'B' Division strugglers Arbroath had previously ousted Hearts at their tiny Gayfield ground and fancied their chances against the Dons. Aberdeen had their own agenda as a history littered with Cup defeats at the semi-final stage was enough incentive for Stan Williams, whose two goals sent Aberdeen through to Hampden.

SATURDAY 13TH APRIL 1929

Alec Cheyne scored the winning goal against England at Hampden Park, direct from a corner kick, in the final minute of the game. Cheyne had plenty to contend with during the match as he lost his team-mate Alec Jackson to injury early in the game. With no substitutes back then, Cheyne was up against it as he was continually outnumbered. He summoned up enough energy in the closing seconds to score the winner. The noise generated by the 110,512 crowd was sustained until the final whistle. Legend has it that was the day the famous 'Hampden Roar' was christened.

TUESDAY 14TH APRIL 1903

The Amalgamation Committee of the three main clubs in the area; Aberdeen, Orion and Victoria United convened at the offices of local solicitor Alex Clarke in Bridge Street to form the present Aberdeen Football Club. A new board of directors were appointed as efforts now turned to gaining admission to the Scottish League. Jimmy Philip was confirmed as manager with Peter Simpson as trainer.

WEDNESDAY 14TH APRIL 1920

Bert MacLachlan received a testimonial for his long service to the club. Former Aberdeen player and Scotland international Wilf Low returned to Pittodrie with a select side that lost 1-0 to the Dons. The game was handled by local referee Peter Craigmyle before a 13,000 attendance.

SATURDAY 14TH APRIL 1984

Ian Porteous and Gordon Strachan scored the goals that took Aberdeen through to the Scottish Cup Final after a 2-0 win over Dundee at Tynecastle. The fiery pitch did little to make this a football spectacle, but Aberdeen were the more competent side throughout and never looked like giving anything away. The Dons were now through to their third Scottish Cup Final in a row; another first for the club.

SATURDAY 14TH APRIL 1990

Two own-goals helped Aberdeen through to the final of the Scottish Cup after a 4-0 win over Dundee United at Tynecastle. Record-signing Hans Gillhaus was inspired as he tormented the United defence all afternoon. Brian Irvine was also on target before a 16,581 crowd.

SATURDAY 15TH APRIL 1882

The first-ever football match played under association rules was contested at the Holburn Cricket grounds. Coupar Angus came north to play the new Aberdeen Football Club on a snowbound pitch. Around 200 spectators were present as the visitors adapted better to the conditions and won 3-1 with the Aberdeen goal coming as a late consolation.

TUESDAY 16TH APRIL 1929

Archie Glen, the former Aberdeen captain was born in Coalburn. Glen, who was spotted by chance by George Hamilton on a visit to his native Ayrshire, went on to become a full international with the Dons after being made captain of the Scotland 'B' team. He was part of the side that won the League and League Cup in 1955 and was made captain after Jimmy Mitchell.

SATURDAY 17TH APRIL 1909

Dundee crushed Aberdeen 9-2 in what is regarded as the worst defeat in the club's history. Contrary to popular belief, the game was actually an Inter-City League tie but was still contested by respective first teams at that time. Many historical references have this result as the worst defeat in the Dons' history.

SATURDAY 17TH APRIL 1971

The destination of the league title was effectively decided at Pittodrie as Aberdeen were held 1-1 by Celtic in the penultimate game of the season. The Reds had been leading the race all season and a win over the Hoops would have clinched the title. Alex Willoughby levelled for Aberdeen before half-time and, but for a goal-line clearance from Celtic captain Billy McNeill after Arthur Graham rounded Evan Williams, Aberdeen would have won their second league championship.

MONDAY 18TH APRIL 1887

The Aberdeenshire FA came into being after a meeting at the Cafe Buildings in Aberdeen. William Jaffray presided and seven members clubs were admitted to form the new Association; Aberdeen, Orion, Caledonian, Aberdeen Rovers, Gladstone, Aberdeen Rangers and Black Diamond. Fixtures were announced and a new Cup – Aberdeenshire Challenge Cup – was presented by Dr F Maitland-Moir.

SATURDAY 19TH APRIL 1947

Frank Dunlop became the first Aberdeen captain to lead the Dons to Scottish Cup success over Hibernian at Hampden Park. They recovered from a disastrous start, conceding a goal in 90 seconds. George Hamilton hauled Aberdeen back on level terms before Stan Williams scored what was described as a "goal in a million" by the local press to take the cup to Pittodrie. He beat two defenders before scoring from an acute angle for a 2-1 win. A crowd of 82,100 welcomed Aberdeen captain Frank Dunlop on to the field to collect the Cup.

SATURDAY 19TH APRIL 1975

The lowest post-war attendance was at Pittodrie – only 3,269 – for the visit of Clyde in wretched weather conditions. Snow storms and blizzards hit the area before kick-off and those that bothered to turn up took refuge in what protection was available from the elements.

SATURDAY 19TH APRIL 1980

A crucial day. Aberdeen travelled to Kilmarnock and won 3-1 with relative ease as news filtered through that Celtic had been beaten 5-1 in Dundee. For the first time in months, the destination of the championship was now in the Dons' own hands.

WEDNESDAY 19TH APRIL 1983

A 1-0 defeat against Waterschei, in Genk, was the Dons' only defeat in the 1982/83 European Cup Winners' Cup competition. A 5-1 success at Pittodrie in the first leg had effectively ended the tie as attention turned to a final date with Real Madrid in Gothenburg. The match in Belgium was the Dons' first European semi-final and even the presentation of confectionery to the Aberdeen players before the start did not deter them from the task in hand.

SUNDAY 20TH APRIL 1986

The first-ever live televised league match in Scotland was honours even with a 1-1 draw against Hearts at Tynecastle. Aberdeen had slipped out of the league race and it was the Edinburgh side who were in the box seat. They could only throw the title away; and they did, some weeks later. Aberdeen looked by far the better side, which was an ominous sign for Hearts as the teams would meet again in the Scottish Cup Final.

SATURDAY 21ST APRIL 1888

Scotland visited the city for the first time and played Aberdeen at the Chanonry in an exhibition match. The local side were no match for the experienced internationals and Scotland were comfortable 6-1 winners. The game attracted huge interest in the area and more than 4,000 filled the tight confines of the small ground. Aberdeen also erected a wooden surround to protect the playing surface before the match. The game was arranged to mark the forming of the Aberdeenshire FA and the new Aberdeenshire Cup. Tom Ketchen scored the Aberdeen goal after Scotland had gone into an early two-goal lead.

MONDAY 21ST APRIL 1947

More than 15,000 turned out to welcome the Aberdeen players home after they won the Scottish Cup against Hibernian. Returning from their Largs base in the evening there were a reported 12,000 supporters standing outside the Joint Station in the pouring rain to catch a glimpse of their heroes. Aberdeen Lord Provost Thomas Mitchell was the first to congratulate the team on their success.

WEDNESDAY 21st APRIL 2004

Injury-hit Aberdeen pulled off the shock result of the Scottish season with a sensational 2-1 win over Celtic at Parkhead. Dons boss Steve Paterson had to turn to some of his under-21 side to answer the call. Celtic had not been beaten at home for 77 games, but David Zdrilic's late goal – after Aberdeen had been under intense pressure – stunned the 51,000 Glasgow crowd.

TUESDAY 22nd APRIL 1912

Peter Simpson was the first Aberdeen trainer in 1903 and was awarded a testimonial by the club when the first team played the reserve side at Pittodrie. A crowd of 1,500 turned out to see the reserves beaten 4-1.

THURSDAY 23rd APRIL 1908

Charlie O'Hagan scored twice as Woolwich Arsenal travelled north to play Aberdeen in a friendly fixture that attracted a 4,000 crowd. The London club were beaten 4-1 and their side included several of their first-team regulars. Aberdeen had previously signed former captain Duncan McNicol from the Arsenal in 1904.

WEDNESDAY 23rd APRIL 1980

Aberdeen went into their decisive game against Celtic knowing that a win would take them a step closer to the league title. Celtic, at one stage, had been 12 points clear, but the Reds had clawed their way back into contention. It was a memorable night for Gordon Strachan as he stamped his class all over the game as Aberdeen came away with a 3-1 win before a passionate 48,000 Celtic support.

SATURDAY 24th APRIL 1937

A British record attendance of 146,433 filled Hampden Park for a first Scottish Cup Final appearance for Aberdeen. Playing in their traditional black and gold strip, Aberdeen eventually went down 2-1 to Celtic, in what was a massive disappointment for the club. Matt Armstrong scored the Aberdeen goal.

SATURDAY 24TH APRIL 1954

The Dons' fourth Scottish Cup Final ended in a 2-1 defeat to Celtic at Hampden Park. An unfortunate own goal by Alex Young proved decisive. Paddy Buckley scored the Aberdeen goal before a 130,060 attendance. The Dons' cause was not helped as both Joe O'Neil and Harry Yorston missed the final through injury.

SATURDAY 24TH APRIL 1976

In the final league game of the season, Aberdeen saved themselves from relegation with a 3-0 win over Hibernian at Pittodrie. The result meant that the Dons finished in seventh place ahead of both Dundee clubs, but defeat could have been disastrous for the Reds. Dave Robb missed an early penalty but Aberdeen nerves were settled when Drew Jarvie scored in 30 minutes.

SATURDAY 25TH APRIL 1959

Favourites Aberdeen were humbled in the Scottish Cup Final at Hampden as St Mirren cruised to a 3-1 win. The Dons had beaten the Buddies with relative ease in both league clashes that season, but a late consolation goal from Hugh Baird was all that Aberdeen had to show for their efforts.

WEDNESDAY 25TH APRIL 1962

Bobby Cummings kept his rich vein of form against Rangers going with a winning goal against the Ibrox side at Pittodrie in the Dons 1-0 win. Cummings had earlier scored three against Rangers and his goal on 49 minutes effectively ended the visitors' hopes of taking the title. Ernie Winchester made his debut as a raw 17-year-old before a 22,000 crowd.

WEDNESDAY 25TH APRIL 1984

The Dons' European Cup Winners' Cup dream was over as Porto won the second leg of the semi-final at Pittodrie. Aberdeen were trailing from the first game in Portugal and when Vermelinho struck in 75 minutes, the Dons hopes of retaining their trophy was gone. At a fog-bound Pittodrie, there were some question marks of the referee who some years later was exposed for taking bribes.

SATURDAY 26TH APRIL 1980

The carnival atmosphere in Aberdeen was enhanced by the fine weather and the annual Aberdeen students' parade at Pittodrie was awash with colour for the visit of St Mirren. It was the Dons last home game of the season and with the club on the threshold of winning the title, Pittodrie was packed with 20,000 fans looking to see their team take another step towards glory. First-half goals from Ian Scanlon and Doug Rougvie were enough to see the Dons take the points.

SATURDAY 27TH APRIL 1907

Newcastle United travelled north to Pittodrie for a friendly fixture that attracted a 9,000 crowd to the Aberdeen ground. The Geordies had been previous visitors to the city winning 7-1. However, a more experienced Dons shocked the English side in a 4-2 win. Wilf Low scored one of the Aberdeen goals and went on to play for the Magpies and Scotland after his transfer in May 1909. On the same day, the Aberdeen reserves won 2-0 at East Stirling in a Dewar Shield tie before a 1,000 crowd.

SATURDAY 27TH APRIL 1985

The Premier League title was won at Pittodrie for the first time after captain Willie Miller scored in the 1-1 draw against nearest challengers Celtic. Aberdeen had also retained the championship for the first time in their history with two games left to play. The Dons would finish seven points clear of Celtic in the final table with a record points haul.

SATURDAY 28TH APRIL 1900

Aberdeen welcomed Glasgow club Celtic to the north-east for a friendly at the new Pittodrie Park. Aberdeen had been through a relatively successful season in local circles but were keen to invite some of the more established clubs from the south. Although it was not the complete Celtic first-team that turned out, the black and golds recorded a fine 4-1 win over Celtic before a 3,000 attendance.

SUNDAY 28TH APRIL 1907

Alec Cheyne, whose famous goals against England at Hampden in 1929 began the 'Hampden Roar', was born in Glasgow. He scored direct from a corner kick in the final moments of that game against England and the ten-men Scots held out to record a memorable victory. Legend has it that the noise generated after the goal from the crowd was sustained until the final whistle and the famed 'Hampden Roar' was born.

SATURDAY 28TH APRIL 1917

Aberdeen finished season 1916/17 with a 2-0 defeat at Morton. The club had been decimated with the war in Europe and the Dons finished bottom of the twenty-team top division. Due to the crippling financial burdens and the loss of most of the first team squad to the military, the club withdrew from competition until the war situation was resolved.

SATURDAY 28TH APRIL 1934

Aberdeen finished their season with a 2-2 draw at home to Queen's Park before a 6,000 crowd. The Dons finished in fifth place with 92 goals from 42 matches, their best return since the prolific days of Benny Yorston and Paddy Moore.

SATURDAY 28TH APRIL 1973

Willie Miller began his Aberdeen career making his debut for the club in the final game of the 1972/73 season. The Dons won 2-1 against Morton at Cappielow and Miller came on in the second period to embark on a memorable Pittodrie career that was to last for 20 years as a player.

SATURDAY 29TH APRIL 1916

Aberdeen brought down the curtain on a troubled season with a 0-0 draw against Rangers at Pittodrie before a poor crowd of 6,000. The Reds finished in 11th place in the league, with Dave Main the top scorer for the fourth year in a row, with 15 goals. The club also had no less than six players serving in the Armed Forces in the war in Europe.

WEDNESDAY 29TH APRIL 1936

Aberdeen completed their season with a stunning 3-2 win over Rangers at Ibrox. The Dons ended in 3rd place, equal on points with Rangers who edged Aberdeen out of the runners-up position. Celtic won the title with 63 points. Aberdeen created a club record 61-point haul, scoring 95 league goals. With 12 Scottish Cup goals scored, Aberdeen bagged 107 goals from their 43 matches; their best ever return since their formation in 1903.

WEDNESDAY 29TH APRIL 1953

Aberdeen lost out to Rangers in the Scottish Cup Final. After a 1-1 draw the teams had to do it all again and the Blues emerged victorious after a 1-0 win before an 113,700 crowd. The Reds had perhaps missed their best chances in the first meeting; Harry Yorston scored for the Dons as they looked the better side in the closing stages.

THURSDAY 29TH APRIL 1965

Eddie Turnbull announced that no less than 17 players were being released as the new Aberdeen manager continued his sweeping changes at the club. Of those players released, the one surprise was that of Andy Kerr who cost the club £8,000 from Sunderland. It was the largest clear-out of staff ever seen at Pittodrie. Bobby Hume and Willie McIntosh were also released days earlier but they were both in South Africa already. Only 19 players were retained.

SATURDAY 29TH APRIL 1967

Aberdeen reached their sixth Scottish Cup Final, only to go down to Celtic in a 2-0 defeat. The Dons cause was not helped by manager Eddie Turnbull being left behind at the team hotel in Gleneagles as he fell ill and was not allowed to travel. The team bus then got caught up in traffic and only arrived 40 minutes before the start. Reds goalkeeper Bobby Clark, who was studying in Glasgow at the time, was the only Aberdeen player at Hampden less than an hour before the start of the game.

TUESDAY 30TH APRIL 1901

Everton made a first visit to Aberdeen, to play at Pittodrie, in a friendly that attracted a crowd of 3,000 to see the established English league side. The home side went into the lead but were eventually undone by the more experienced visitors in a 3-2 defeat.

SATURDAY 30TH APRIL 1904

Newcastle United were the first English side to play Aberdeen after the amalgamation of 1903. United proved too strong for Aberdeen as they ran out comfortable 7-1 winners in a friendly match that attracted a crowd of 5,000. The game was seen by Aberdeen as an ideal test and one that could gauge their hopes of getting into the mainstream Scottish game.

WEDNESDAY 30TH APRIL 1924

Jock Hutton received his benefit game from Aberdeen as Liverpool travelled north to play the Dons at Pittodrie. Hutton was well known for his thunderous shot and his unique style at scoring penalties. Not many goalkeepers would stand up to him. His testimonial attracted a 6,000 crowd to Pittodrie as Aberdeen drew 1-1 with the Anfield side. Hutton was a Scotland regular and went on to join Huddersfield in a record £5,000 deal.

TUESDAY 30TH APRIL 1946

Airdrie took Aberdeen to a replay in their Southern League Cup semi-final at Ibrox. After a 2-2 draw in the first game, the sides met again three days later. A crowd of 45,000 turned out to see the Dons make it to the Hampden Park final after a 5-3 win over the Broomfield side. Once again the game went into extra time and two goals from Alec Kiddie helped Aberdeen through to meet Rangers in the first post-war final. The Dons could do little wrong in cup competitions as their efforts during war-time football was put to good use.

ABERDEEN FC
On This Day

MAY

THURSDAY 1st MAY 1919

South African winger Stan Williams was born in Johannesburg. Williams was spotted by the Aberdeen touring party in 1937, and although he joined the club a year later, his career at Pittodrie did not really begin until after the war. It was against Hibernian in the 1947 Scottish Cup Final that Williams attained legendary status after scoring the winning goal that took the trophy to Pittodrie for the first time. Williams went on to play for Plymouth and Dundee before retiring in 1952.

MONDAY 2nd MAY 1955

Legendary Aberdeen captain Willie Miller was born in Glasgow. Miller joined Aberdeen from Eastercraigs in June 1971 to begin a remarkable association with the club. It was Miller who was the captain through the Dons' golden era in the 1980s, and beyond. After playing more than 700 times for the club, Miller went on to coach and manage at Pittodrie before returning to join the board in June 2004, a position he retains to this day.

WEDNESDAY 2nd MAY 1984

Stewart McKimmie scored his first goal for the club as Aberdeen clinched the Premier League title against Hearts at Tynecastle. The Dons still had four games left to complete the formality after building up a sizeable lead throughout the season. More than 6,000 Aberdeen supporters made their way to Edinburgh for the game.

SATURDAY 3rd MAY 1980

The Old Firm domination of the league was broken when Aberdeen clinched the Premier League title after a 5-0 win at relegated Hibernian. The Dons had to win and hope that Celtic slipped up against St Mirren. The Reds had clawed their way back into contention after two crucial wins over Celtic in Glasgow. Aberdeen cruised to a comfortable victory, while news filtered through from Paisley that Celtic had been held by the Love Street side. Alex Ferguson ran on to the pitch and celebrated with his players as the 8,000 travelling Red Army joined in the fun.

SATURDAY 3RD MAY 1986

Aberdeen eased past Clydebank in the final game of the season with a 6-0 win at Kilbowie. Several squad players were given their chance as Alex Ferguson saved his big guns for the Scottish Cup Final seven days later. The Reds finished in a disappointing fourth place. As Aberdeen were going through the motions against Clydebank, it was all happening at Dens Park where Hearts lost the title in the final seven minutes of their game against Dundee.

SATURDAY 4TH MAY 1907

Aberdeen won the Dewar Shield for the first time after a comfortable 3-0 win over St Johnstone at Pittodrie. It was the Dons' reserve side that contested the final as the first team were on league duty against Queen's Park that day. Alf Ward scored two of the Aberdeen goals in a final that was well attended by the Pittodrie faithful.

FRIDAY 4TH MAY 1951

South African winger Billy Strauss was rewarded for his loyalty with a testimonial match between Plymouth Argyle and Aberdeen that took place at Holm Park. The crowd of 12,000 were treated to a feast of football in a 2-2 draw. George Hamilton scored both Aberdeen goals and his side should have won the game in the closing stages, hitting the post. Shortt pulled off two great saves for the home side.

SATURDAY 4TH MAY 1985

Unlucky 13 for Hearts. That's how long it took for Frank McDougall to hit three goals past a hapless Henry Smith in the opponents' goal. Aberdeen had clinched the league title with two games left and they turned on the style to embarrass the Tynecastle side in front of their own supporters. McDougall celebrated his first season with Aberdeen by finishing as the top scorer in the Premier. His third goal was a sublime volley, after he had lobbed the ball over a Hearts defender.

THURSDAY 5TH MAY 1983

As Aberdeen prepared for their European Cup Winners' Cup Final date with Real Madrid in Gothenburg, the Dons last league game before the final was brought forward by two days. Kilmarnock were the visitors as the team turned in an impressive display with a 5-0 win over an already doomed Rugby Park side. John McMaster was among the goals and his 39th minute goal was also the Dons' 500th in the Premier league.

MONDAY 6TH MAY 1902

As the football season came to a close in Aberdeen, a flurry of friendlies were played out in the area. Hearts visited Pittodrie and emerged victorious in a 5-2 win over the 'Whites', while down at Central Park, a Rangers side travelled north to play Victoria United and eased past them in a 7-0 win.

SATURDAY 6TH MAY 1978

As Scotland prepared to travel to Argentina for the World Cup, Aberdeen lost to Rangers in the Scottish Cup Final… a bitter disappointment. The Dons had gone 23 games unbeaten in the build up to the final but they effectively 'froze' on the day and Billy McNeill's only season in charge was to end in defeat.

SATURDAY 6TH MAY 1995

Dundee United visited Pittodrie in what was one of the most important matches in the Dons' history. After a season where Aberdeen had parted company with Willie Miller as manager, the Dons looked certain to be relegated for the first time in their history after a succession of poor results. However, the Dons would go on to win their final five matches to survive. Goals from Billy Dodds and Duncan Shearer gave Aberdeen a 2-1 win and condemned United to relegation.

FRIDAY 7TH MAY 1937

South Africa was the destination for an Aberdeen touring party which set sail from Southampton on the Stirling Castle steam ship.

TUESDAY 7TH MAY 1985

One of the most remarkable comebacks at Pittodrie. The Aberdeen youth side beat Celtic 5-3 to win the BP Youth Cup. The Aberdeen first team squad were present to collect the Premier League trophy before the game, and a 6,500 crowd. After 65 minutes, the young Dons looked down and out as they trailed 3-0. After captain Paul Wright clawed a goal back in the 66th minute, the Reds showed real spirit to take the final into extra time when Joe Miller levelled the tie at 3-3 in the closing minutes. Two extra-time goals for the Dons completed the comeback.

FRIDAY 8TH MAY 1936

George Mulhall, the Aberdeen winger who went on to play for Scotland, was born. Mulhall had to be patient in his Dons career before he finally replaced Jackie Hather in the side. After being capped for Scotland in October 1959, he went on to play 150 games for Aberdeen, scoring 42 goals. In September 1962 he was sold to Sunderland.

MONDAY 9TH MAY 1983

As preparations for the Dons' European Cup Winners' Cup Final date with Real Madrid entered the final stages, around 500 Dons supporters set sail on the St Clair ferry from Aberdeen heading for Gothenburg. The ferry, which was normally used for commuting between the Shetland Isles, was taken over for the week by what became known as the 'Red Armada'. The trip would take 27 hours and would not return to Aberdeen until Friday afternoon.

SUNDAY 10TH MAY 1903

Hopes of Aberdeen being admitted to the First Division of the league were dealt a hammer blow with another refusal. Despite having the backing of some of the senior clubs in Scotland, the new club were left devastated by the decision. With no application to join the Second Division being made, Aberdeen had to be content with a season in the Northern League.

WEDNESDAY 10TH MAY 1911

Aberdeen embarked on their first foreign tour, taking in Bohemia and Poland; a journey which back then took the best part of four days by rail, sea and road. Dons had finished as league runners-up and the trip proved a success as the touring party were received well on their travels. They became the first Scottish club to travel to Eastern Europe.

SATURDAY 10TH MAY 1986

Aberdeen won the Scottish Cup for the sixth time after an impressive 3-0 win over Heart of Midlothian at Hampden Park before a 62,841 attendance. The Edinburgh side had lost out in the title seven days earlier in dramatic fashion and an experienced Aberdeen side inflicted further misery on their opponents. The Dons cruised to victory and never looked back after John Hewitt scored in the opening minutes.

SATURDAY 11TH MAY 1946

It was a first national trophy for Aberdeen as they defeated Rangers 3-2 to win the Southern League Cup at Hampden Park. Sun-drenched conditions made the Dons' free-flowing game more difficult but they snatched victory in the last minute when George Taylor converted an Alec Kiddie cross from 12 yards. More than 135,000 filled Hampden for what was the first major final since the end of hostilities in Europe. An estimated 50,000 lined the streets of Aberdeen as the players returned in triumph.

WEDNESDAY 11TH MAY 1983

Aberdeen's finest hour; the Dons won the European Cup Winners' Cup after a memorable 2-1 victory over Real Madrid in the Ullevi Stadium in Gothenburg. Over 15,000 Aberdeen supporters made their way to Sweden by all means possible. In torrential rain their heroes took the lead through Eric Black after he beat Augustin from close range. Juanito restored parity in 14 minutes after Santillana was brought down by Jim Leighton. The Reds dominated the rest of the game, eventually prevailing in extra time. Mark McGhee crossed for John Hewitt to head the winning goal.

SATURDAY 11TH MAY 1991

A defining moment in Aberdeen FC history; following a remarkable unbeaten run, the Dons went to Ibrox for the final game of the season looking for a point to take the League title. Rookie keeper Michael Watt was thrown into the side and after Mark Hateley put Rangers ahead early in the game there was no way back for Aberdeen. Manager Alex Smith was heavily criticised following this defeat; he was eventually sacked in February 1992.

FRIDAY 12TH MAY 1905

Alex Jackson of 'Wembley Wizard' fame was born in Renton. Jackson joined Aberdeen in 1924 after he was spotted by Jock Hume in America. Capped for Scotland at 19 years of age, Jackson only graced Pittodrie for one season before signing for Huddersfield in a record £5,000 transfer. Jackson was in the Scotland side that defeated England at Wembley in 1928 and scored a hat-trick in the Scots 5-1 victory.

SUNDAY 12TH MAY 1924

Aberdeen embarked on a short tour of Eastern Germany, playing three matches. Against Dresden, the Dons won 3-1. A day earlier, the Dons had defeated Magdeburg 4-2 before a 6,000 crowd. The trip was completed with a 3-1 defeat against English side Bolton in Leipzig.

THURSDAY 12TH MAY 1983

Jubilant scenes as the Aberdeen players returned home after winning the European Cup Winners' Cup against Real Madrid in Sweden. The players went through the city on an open-topped bus parade that culminated in 22,000 waiting inside Pittodrie to greet the conquering heroes. An estimated 100,000 took to the streets.

SATURDAY 12TH MAY 1990

"Like shooting ducks at the fair," was Aberdeen manager Alex Smith's post-match assessment after the club had defeated Celtic 9-8 in a first-ever Scottish Cup Final penalty shoot-out. A disappointing game ended 0-0 and it was down to Dons centre-half Brian Irvine who scored the decisive spot-kick. Dutch keeper Theo Snelders had saved an Anton Rogan kick to set Aberdeen up for victory.

SATURDAY 13TH MAY 1899

Orion were crowned Northern League champions after a 1-0 win over Dundee Wanderers at Arbroath's Gayfield ground. Orion led from the front and were leaders in the title race all season and followed up their 4-2 win over Wanderers at Cattofield in April to clinch the title in their final league game.

MONDAY 13TH MAY 1901

Aberdeen made an application to join the Scottish League following a successful season in the north-east where crowds had substantially increased. The Dundee Telegraph also carried a report in that both Paisley and Kilmarnock boasted of having teams in the top league and they were a far smaller population base than Aberdeen.

SATURDAY 13TH MAY 1911

Slavia Prague were beaten 2-1 by Aberdeen on the club's first foreign tour. Jock Hume scored both Aberdeen goals. Hume was a full-back who on occasion was used in a forward's role. He also took the occasional penalty for the club.

MONDAY 13TH MAY 1929

Fred Martin, the Aberdeen and Scotland goalkeeper, was born in Carnoustie. Martin joined Aberdeen from Carnoustie Panmure in 1946 as an inside-forward but it was during a stint in the National Service that he returned to Pittodrie as a first-class goalkeeper. Martin was the first Scotland goalkeeper to play in the World Cup Finals, in Switzerland in 1954. A year later he was celebrating with Aberdeen as league champions and League Cup winners. Martin played 291 games for the Dons before retiring in 1961.

SATURDAY 13TH MAY 1989

Rangers' title party was spoiled by Aberdeen on the final day of the season. Aberdeen finished their campaign in style with a 3-0 win at Ibrox, before a 42,480 crowd. Rangers were getting presented with the league trophy after the game but it was Aberdeen that took the plaudits to ruin the celebrations.

SATURDAY 13TH MAY 1995

The final league game of the season was a vital one for Aberdeen as they continued their battle to escape relegation. Goals from Scott Thomson and Stephen Glass gave the Dons a 2-0 win at Falkirk, urged on by a travelling Red Army of 8,000. The result put Aberdeen through to a first-ever Premier League play-off as Dundee United were virtually relegated.

SUNDAY 14TH MAY 1876

Rab MacFarlane, the renowned Aberdeen goalkeeper, was born in Greenock. MacFarlane was a real character and was known for his conversations with supporters behind his goal in the quiet moments of a game. Previously with Celtic, MacFarlane joined Aberdeen in July 1904. His colourful career at Pittodrie came to an end in 1908 after claims that he had 'gifted' a goal to Celtic in the semi-final of the Scottish Cup. After a spell with Motherwell, and in Australia, he eventually returned to Greenock to open a confectionery shop.

SUNDAY 14TH MAY 1911

Aberdeen became the first provincial side in Scotland to play abroad when they took on Slavia Prague. The touring party hardly had time to get used to the dramatic change in weather conditions and Prague defeated the Scots 3-2 before an enthusiastic home crowd. The Aberdeen players later highlighted the hot weather conditions as something that they were not used to. While their hosts were perhaps quicker on the ball, it was the Scots that surprised the home fans with their skill.

SUNDAY 15TH MAY 1977

Yugoslavia was the Dons' destination for an obscure friendly against OFK Kikinda. It was significant in that it was Ally MacLeod's last game in charge of Aberdeen before he decided to take over as Scotland coach. Jim Leighton also made his first appearance for the Dons. With regular goalkeepers Bobby Clark and Ally MacLean both injured, third choice John Gardiner did not have a passport which meant that young Leighton had to fill the breach.

SATURDAY 15TH MAY 1982

Aberdeen took the title race down to the final game of the season, thanks a long unbeaten run. There was still an outside chance as the Dons had to beat Rangers 5-0 while hoping that Celtic would slip up at home to St Mirren. By half-time the impossible dream was on as Aberdeen had raced into a 4-0 lead over Rangers as Celtic were being held by St Mirren. The Dons could not add to their tally but the win was a boost for the Scottish Cup Final against Rangers a week later.

WEDNESDAY 16TH MAY 1990

Scotland prepared for the World Cup Finals in Italy with a disappointing 3-1 defeat against Egypt at Pittodrie. The result was the first occasion that the national side had lost in the city. Former Aberdeen goalkeeper Bryan Gunn was in the side and the Dons had Alex McLeish, Jim Bett and Stewart McKimmie in the line-up. Ally McCoist scored a consolation goal before an all-ticket 23,000 crowd. All three Aberdeen players would travel to Italy for the finals.

WEDNESDAY 17TH MAY 1905

Aberdeen had the embarrassment of losing to their reserve side in the final of the Fleming Shield at Pittodrie as the 1904/05 season drew to a close. The tradition back then was for the match to be the last game of the season. With both sides getting through, the 3,000 crowd saw the reserves win 3-1 with Knowles, Caie and Hamilton scoring the goals.

SATURDAY 18TH MAY 1901

Orion lost out to Dundee 'A' at Dens Park in what was a deciding game for the Northern League championship. The Aberdeen side went down 3-0 before 3,000 fans. It completed a bad week for Orion who lost the Rhodesia Cup Final to Victoria United earlier in the week.

SATURDAY 19TH MAY 1984

Celtic were beaten 2-1 as Aberdeen made it an historic three Scottish Cup wins in succession. Once again it took the Reds an extra time period to see off the Celtic challenge. Mark McGhee scored the winning goal in what was his final appearance for the Dons before moving to Hamburg. With Aberdeen also winning the championship, it was a first League and Cup double in the club's history.

JOHN HEWITT SCORES THE THIRD GOAL IN A 4-0 WIN OVER RANGERS IN MAY 1982

FRIDAY 19TH MAY 1995

Roy Aitken was appointed Aberdeen manager at a time when the Dons top-flight status looked precarious. After a succession of defeats in the league, Aberdeen parted company with Willie Miller and turned to his former assistant Aitken in a desperate move to halt the decline. Aitken had been a fierce rival to the Dons in his playing days but he was able to muster a side that battled to the end and eventually saved the club's status through a first-ever league play-off against First Division runners-up Dunfermline.

SATURDAY 20TH MAY 1911

Aberdeen were in Poland on their tour of Eastern Europe and defeated Wisla Krakow 9-1 with Jock Hume scoring five of their goals and top scorer Dave Main netting four.

SUNDAY 20TH MAY 1951

George Hamilton became the first Aberdeen player to score three times for Scotland in a full international when his country humbled Belgium 5-0 in Brussels. 'Gentleman' George, as he was known, scored in the 8th, 65th and 81st minute before a 55,135 crowd.

TUESDAY 20TH MAY 2003

Gordon Strachan took his Southampton side to Pittodrie as part of the Dons' Centenary celebrations, two days after the Saints lost to Arsenal in the FA Cup Final in Cardiff. Strachan played his part in the Dons halcyon era of the 1980s. The home side completed their season with a 2-1 win with goals from Jamie McAllister and Leigh Hinds.

SUNDAY 20TH MAY 2006

Rangers visited Pittodrie in the final game of the season with Aberdeen looking for the victory that would secure a Uefa Cup place. The all-ticket capacity crowd bathed in the sunshine as goals from Scott Severin and Steve Lovell brought European football back to Pittodrie at the expense of Hearts, who went down at Kilmarnock.

MONDAY 21st MAY 1906

Scotland international Frank Hill was born in Forfar. After joining Aberdeen in 1924, 'Tiger' Hill, as he became known, played more than 100 games for Aberdeen before he was implicated in the 'Great Mystery' betting scandal that rocked the club in November 1931. Hill was sold to Arsenal and was part of the Gunners' side that won three league titles in succession between 1932 and 1935. Hill went on to manage the Iraqi national side in 1957, among others, before retiring after a spell as a scout at Manchester City.

SUNDAY 21st MAY 1972

Aberdeen were on tour to the USA, in the close season, and defeated Wolverhampton 3-1 in San Francisco. The game was watched by many ex-pats and the crowd of around 8,000 saw Aberdeen play with real style against a strong Wolves side that included former Don Frank Munro. Joe Harper scored twice; his second a superb volley from 25 yards. Willie Young was awarded the man-of-the-match after he managed to keep the dangerous John Richards quiet throughout the game.

SATURDAY 21st MAY 1983

A memorable season for Aberdeen came to a close with a 1-0 victory over Rangers that meant that Dons had retained the Scottish Cup for the first time. Alex Ferguson was livid after the final whistle as he berated his players' performance despite the win that was the Dons 60th competitive game of the season. Always seeking perfection, and with the European Cup Winners' Cup already won, Ferguson later apologised to his players. Eric Black's winning goal was also the Dons 600th in the Scottish Cup.

SUNDAY 21st MAY 1995

A massive game for Aberdeen as a packed Pittodrie was not the venue that First Division side Dunfermline Athletic would have expected to visit for their play-off match. The stadium was a hostile place as the Dons were battling for their survival. Two goals from Duncan Shearer put Aberdeen in control – and a 3-1 lead – to take to East End Park for the return leg.

MONDAY 22ND MAY 1905

A meeting of the Scottish League committee, held in their West George Street premises, was an important one for Aberdeen as they were finally admitted to the First Division. Manager Jimmy Philip had championed the Aberdeen cause for many months and his efforts were rewarded after a motion from Celtic to increase the size of the First Division was carried. The Dons were admitted along with Falkirk even though Clyde had won the championship. It has been a position they have held ever since.

SATURDAY 22ND MAY 1943

Stan Mortensen of FA Cup Final fame was a regular in the Aberdeen side during the war period. Mortensen was always a star attraction and against the British Army side at Linksfield Stadium he scored all four Aberdeen goals in a 5-4 defeat. The nearby Linksfield ground was used for the hurriedly arranged game because Pittodrie was being utilised as a munitions dump during the hostilities.

SATURDAY 22ND MAY 1982

The Scottish Cup came north for the third time after Aberdeen beat old rival Rangers 4-1 at Hampden Park. Despite falling behind, the Dons levelled through a superb goal from Alex McLeish. It took extra-time for Aberdeen to finally stamp their class on the game; Neale Cooper scored from all of two yards in the closing minutes to complete a day of misery for Rangers. This win earned Aberdeen entry into the 1982/83 European Cup Winners' Cup.

THURSDAY 22ND MAY 2008

The final game of the SPL season attracted a capacity crowd to Pittodrie for the visit of Rangers. With Aberdeen out of contention for Europe, Rangers could have won the title had Celtic slipped up at Dundee United. As it was, the Dons had their own agenda and second-half goals from Lee Miller and Darren Mackie ensured that there would be no Ibrox celebrations. The win moved Aberdeen up to a fourth place finish that looked well beyond them at one stage.

TUESDAY 23RD MAY 1911

Incredible scenes as the Aberdeen touring party were asked to play local sides Prerau and Brunn during their tour of Eastern Europe. The Dons players had to get off their train en route to the closing games of the tour when the locals insisted on Aberdeen playing them. They were well received and Aberdeen went on to beat Prerau 8-0, then Brunn 6-1.

SUNDAY 23RD MAY 1976

Aberdeen starlet Stephen Glass was born in Dundee. Glass emerged in the side that was struggling to retain their top-flight status in 1995. It soon became clear that Glass was a player of huge potential and that was realised with his man-of-the-match performance in the 1995 League Cup Final. Glass was sold to Newcastle after a tribunal set a fee of £650,000 for his sale.

THURSDAY 24TH MAY 1956

Doug Rougvie, the Aberdeen and Scotland defender was born in Ballingry, Fife. Rougvie joined Aberdeen in 1972 and spent most of his early years in the reserves before becoming a part of the side that had enjoyed so much success in the 1980s. It was a controversial red card received in the 1979 League Cup Final against Rangers that inadvertently endeared him to the Aberdeen support. Rougvie went on to become a colossus in the side with his physical presence and 'no-prisoners' approach.

MONDAY 24TH MAY 1965

Brian Irvine, the Aberdeen and Scotland centre-half was born in Bellshill. Irvine was brought to Pittodrie by Alex Ferguson in 1985 from Falkirk. After making 338 appearances for the Reds, he moved to Dundee after being released by the Dons in 1997. In between times, Irvine won nine Scotland caps and was also on target in the crucial 1990 Scottish Cup Final shoot-out, scoring the decisive goal that took the Cup north.

THURSDAY 25TH MAY 1995

Aberdeen completed their great escape act against Dunfermline Athletic at East End Park in the return leg of their Premier League play-off. Leading 3-1 from the first game at Pittodrie, the Reds took 8,000 supporters down to Fife for the return. The Dons won 3-1, completing a 6-2 aggregate win.

SATURDAY 26TH MAY 1984

Mark McGhee was on target for Scotland against England in the 1-1 draw at Hampden. Seven days earlier he scored the winning goal that took the Scottish Cup to Pittodrie, on his last appearance for the club. McGhee completed his move to SV Hamburg in the German Bundesliga before the new season began.

SATURDAY 26TH MAY 2000

Jim Leighton's final competitive appearance for Aberdeen was short-lived as the legendary Dons goalkeeper was injured in the opening minutes of the Scottish Cup Final against Rangers. With no substitute listed, it was outfield player Robbie Winters that faced Rangers for the duration of the game. A 4-0 win for Rangers was no surprise; the rules were swiftly changed in the aftermath of this game to allow teams to include a substitute goalkeeper.

FRIDAY 27TH MAY 1938

Aberdeen were invited along with Celtic, Rangers and Hearts to represent Scotland in the Empire Exhibition Cup. Brentford, Chelsea, Everton and Sunderland made up the English contingent. Aberdeen came up against Chelsea in the opening match and the Dons turned in one of their finest performances of the season in a 4-0 win before a 22,000 crowd at Ibrox.

MONDAY 27TH MAY 1963

The Dons had to wait three weeks to complete their season due to Rangers' cup commitments. After such a promising start, the end could not come quick enough for the Dons who had exited the Scottish Cup and fallen away in the league. Despite the prolonged break, the Dons managed to hold league winners Rangers in a 2-2 draw that saw Aberdeen finish the season in sixth place.

TUESDAY 27TH MAY 1986

Chris Anderson, the Aberdeen player and latterly director, lost his battle against motor neurone disease after a long illness. Anderson was a schoolboy international that gave Aberdeen great service as a player before joining the board in 1967. It was as a director that he excelled.

SUNDAY 28TH MAY 1911

Aberdeen completed a ground-breaking tour of Eastern Europe with a 4-1 win over Czech side Pardubitz. The eight-game tour lasted 17 days, and after losing the first game to Slavia Prague, the Dons won all their other matches.

FRIDAY 28TH MAY 2004

Jimmy Calderwood was appointed Aberdeen manager after new Dons director Willie Miller had negotiated a deal to bring Calderwood and his assistant Jimmy Nicholl to Pittodrie. The duo had taken Dunfermline Athletic into Europe, but Calderwood was tempted by joining a bigger club and he kept Aberdeen in the SPL top six in his first three seasons in charge.

SATURDAY 29TH MAY 1993

With Hampden Park under construction, the Scottish Cup Final was moved to Celtic Park. Aberdeen, looking to halt Rangers' treble bid, went down 2-1 with Lee Richardson scoring the Dons' goal.

THURSDAY 30TH MAY 1940

The Scottish football authorities announced that due to the war in Europe, and the increase in hostilities, all football would cease to be played for the entire 1940/41 season. With Pittodrie being used as a munitions dump all attentions were focused on the war effort.

TUESDAY 30TH MAY 1967

Legendary talent spotter Bobby Calder was the subject of a cheeky bid by Rangers to prise him away from Aberdeen. With the Dons on tour in the USA, it was left to Calder to endorse his position with the club: "I will not be quitting Aberdeen. I gave Eddie Turnbull my word that I would not leave Aberdeen and I will always stick by that". Calder went on to bring a host of young talent to Pittodrie.

THURSDAY 30TH MAY 1968

Bobby Clark made his second Scotland appearance when he played against Holland in the Olympic Stadium in Amsterdam. Clark was inspired in a 0-0 draw before a 19,000 attendance.

MONDAY 31ST MAY 1937

Willie Mills scored one of the Aberdeen goals as the Dons defeated Northern Transvaal 2-0 during their tour of South Africa. This was the club's fourth straight win and 6,000 turned out to see the Scots in Pretoria. Included in the Aberdeen side were South African-born Herbert Currer and Billy Strauss.

WEDNESDAY 31ST MAY 1967

Aberdeen won their second game of the President's Cup in the USA when the Washington Whips defeated Hibernian (Toronto City) 2-1 in the Varsity Stadium in Toronto. Aberdeen played in an all-white kit and the 12,000 supporters were treated to what was described by local journalists as the "best game seen in Toronto for ten years".

TUESDAY 31ST MAY 1988

Alex Smith was appointed Aberdeen manager after Ian Porterfield's resignation. Smith had previously been with Stirling Albion and was part of a new set up at Pittodrie that also saw Jocky Scott appointed as co-manager. Another former Don Drew Jarvie completed the new managerial set up by becoming assistant manager in charge of the reserve and youth teams.

MONDAY 31ST MAY 1999

Brondby coach Ebbe Skovdahl became the first foreign Aberdeen manager as he took over from Paul Hegarty. Skovdahl first came to the attention of the Reds with his Brondby side that had eliminated the club from the Uefa Cup in 1996. Reported to be on a salary in excess of £300,000 a year, Skovdahl's first season in charge saw Aberdeen finish at the foot of the SPL yet reach both domestic cup finals. His popularity never seemed to wane despite presiding over some of the worst results in the club's history.

ABERDEEN FC
On This Day

JUNE

WEDNESDAY 1st JUNE 1983

Four Aberdeen players were selected to play for Scotland against England at Wembley. Jim Leighton, Willie Miller, Alex McLeish and Gordon Strachan all started for the Scots.

FRIDAY 1st JUNE 1984

Willie Miller was made captain of Scotland for the trip to face Marseille in France. Miller was one of five Aberdeen players in the starting line-up against a side on the threshold of European success. The Dons legend was joined by Jim Leighton, Alex McLeish, Gordon Strachan and Neil Simpson. The Reds went down 2-0. Strachan was soon to complete his move to Manchester United.

MONDAY 2nd JUNE 1924

Jimmy Philip stood down as Aberdeen boss after 21 years in charge. Philip had been the driving force behind the club for many years and it was his exhaustive lobbying inside the Scottish League that eventually ensured Aberdeen were admitted to the league.

SATURDAY 2nd JUNE 1945

Jock Pattillo was on the mark for Aberdeen with two goals in a 3-1 win over Raith Rovers at Pittodrie. The Mitchell Cup was competed for by east coast sides during the war. The trophy was donated by Aberdeen chairman James Mitchell.

FRIDAY 2nd JUNE 1978

It was the beginning of a new era at Aberdeen as Alex Ferguson became boss. Ferguson had left St Mirren to take over as successor to Billy McNeill and began his coaching career with East Stirling before taking the Love Street outfit to the Premier League. Ferguson was welcomed officially to Pittodrie by chairman Dick Donald and Chris Anderson.

WEDNESDAY 2nd JUNE 1993

Scotland played their seventh full international at Pittodrie, winning 3-1 over Estonia in a World Cup qualifier. The poor crowd of 14,500 was down to Aberdeen losing the Scottish Cup Final four days previously. Pat Nevin scored twice with Stewart McKimmie, Brian Irvine and Scott Booth completing the Aberdeen representation.

SATURDAY 3RD JUNE 1967

The 'Washington Whips', as Aberdeen were known, were touring the USA and came up against Italian side Cagliari. Jim Storrie scored the Dons goal in a 1-1 draw.

SUNDAY 4TH JUNE 1967

Cagliari, under the guise of Chicago Mustangs, held Aberdeen to a 1-1 draw in the Presidents' Cup in the USA. The game was played in the DC Stadium in Washington. Italian international Boninsegna put Chicago ahead and it took a double penalty save from Bobby Clark shortly after to keep Aberdeen in the game. The hot conditions played their part as the players struggled in the searing heat. Only 6,125 turned out to see the match. It wasn't short of incident with Boninsegna being sent off after throwing a punch at Aberdeen scorer Jim Storrie.

SUNDAY 4TH JUNE 1972

Ecuador champions Barcelona were beaten 5-1 by Aberdeen as the Dons ended a poor sequence of results on their summer tour to Canada. The game was played in Randall's Island in New York and 2,000 turned out to see Aberdeen turn in their best performance of the tour. Despite the temperature touching 85 degrees, four goals in 21 minutes helped the Dons to an easy win against a side that were as physical as the Reds had met all season.

WEDNESDAY 4TH JUNE 1986

Alex Ferguson continued in his dual role of managing Aberdeen and Scotland by leading his country to the World Cup Finals in Mexico. Scotland opened with a 1-0 defeat against Denmark in Neza. Jim Leighton, Alex McLeish and Willie Miller from Aberdeen were all in the starting XI.

SATURDAY 5TH JUNE 1937

Johnny Lang and Willie Mills were among the goals as Aberdeen were defeated by Natal in Durban during the club's end-of-season tour to South Africa in 1937. The 4-3 defeat was their first of the tour after five matches.

SUNDAY 5TH JUNE 1938

After defeating Chelsea in the opening match of the Empire Exhibition Cup at Ibrox, Aberdeen were disappointed to go down 3-2 against a strong Everton side in their semi-final clash. Goals from Matt Armstrong and Billy Strauss were not enough to put Aberdeen through to the final. Everton lost to Celtic some days later.

SATURDAY 6TH JUNE 1942

In the last North Eastern League fixture of the season during the war, Aberdeen crushed Dundee United 6-1 at Pittodrie to complete a successful season in what was a regional league set up. Stan Williams and Matt Armstrong were among the Dons scorers.

THURSDAY 7TH JUNE 1956

Aberdeen recorded their biggest victory in all matches with an incredible 17-0 win over Regina during their tour of Canada. The long list of scorers included Graham Leggat with four goals, while Willie Allan and Paddy Buckley scored three each.

WEDNESDAY 7TH JUNE 1967

Jimmy Smith was on target as Aberdeen defeated Cerro 3-0 on tour in America. This was classed as a 'home' game for the Dons as it was played in Washington, which was the adopted name of the Dons for the duration of their stay. Cerro, from Montevideo in Uruguay, were playing under their adopted name of the New York Skyliners. The Uruguayans showed the ugly side of football with their cynical approach. Dave Johnston had to be taken to hospital after a late tackle caused an injury to his leg that required 20 stitches.

SUNDAY 8TH JUNE 1986

Jim Leighton and Willie Miller were in the Scotland side that stretched Germany in a World Cup tie in Queretaro in Mexico. Former Don Gordon Strachan scored for Scotland in a 2-1 defeat. Scotland gave a good account of themselves in the game and Strachan will always be remembered for his goal 'celebration' when he struggled to hurdle the advertising boarding after his strike.

SATURDAY 9TH JUNE 1956

Everton and Aberdeen clashed on four occasions while both clubs were on tour to Canada. In the first meeting in Vancouver, two goals from Jackie Hather helped Aberdeen to a 3-3 draw. This exhibition match attracted a crowd of 18,382 to the Empire Stadium and was also one of the first to be played under the relatively new concept of floodlights, in Canada.

WEDNESDAY 9TH JUNE 1971

Bobby Clark became the most capped player in Aberdeen history when he played against Denmark in Copenhagen. His eighth appearance bettered Jock Hutton's seven-cap haul in 1923. Goalkeeper Clark went on to make 17 appearances for Scotland, who lost 1-0 to the Danes. Jim Forrest and Dave Robb were the other Aberdeen players in the side.

THURSDAY 9TH JUNE 1977

Celtic hero Billy McNeill was appointed Aberdeen manager to replace Ally MacLeod who had taken over as Scotland coach. McNeill was the first British player to lead his side to a European Cup success. The Dons had taken him from his first managerial post at Clyde after he retired from playing immediately after the 1975 Scottish Cup Final. McNeill took Aberdeen to the brink of success in his one and only season at Pittodrie before taking over at his beloved Celtic.

SATURDAY 10TH JUNE 1972

Aberdeen completed their tour of Canada with a comfortable 5-0 win over Boston Astros in Boston. Jim Forrest, Dave Robb, Drew Jarvie and Joe Harper were all on the mark for the tourists. While the Dons had moved on from the heat of New York, it was a different story in Boston where the game was played in freezing evening temperatures. A crowd of 3,500 watched Aberdeen complete their tour in style, although many of the games were played on Astroturf which most of the players did not find to their liking.

SUNDAY 11TH JUNE 1967

Irish side Glentoran held Aberdeen to a 2-2 draw in America. The Irish side were known as the Detroit Cougars and goals from Jimmy Wilson and Pat Wilson kept Aberdeen on course for qualifying for the final of the Presidents' Cup. The Dons were now heading for a clash against nearest rivals Stoke City. The Whips were fortunate to escape with a point from the clash in the University Stadium as fatigue played a big part in the Dons' struggle to match the pace of their hosts.

FRIDAY 12TH JUNE 1992

Scotland opened their European Championship finals campaign with a 1-0 defeat against Holland. The game was played in the Ullevi Stadium in Gothenburg, scene of the Dons' 1983 epic European Cup Winners' Cup triumph. Stewart McKimmie was the only Aberdeen player involved in the Scotland side, who lost to Germany and defeated the CIS in their final game.

SUNDAY 13TH JUNE 1937

Lourenco Marques provided the opposition on the Dons' South African tour. The game was played on a Sunday in what was one of the first occasions an Aberdeen side had done so. The 6-4 win saw Armstrong, Benyon and Devine among the goals. The game was played in front of a small crowd in Mozambique.

WEDNESDAY 14TH JUNE 1967

Cleveland Stokers, better known as Stoke City, held Aberdeen to a 2-2 draw in Cleveland as the Dons clocked up the air miles during their tour of America. This was far from a friendly with both sides being involved in some nasty incidents throughout the game. Dons were two points behind Stoke at the top of the Eastern section and many thought that they would have to win to maintain their interest. At half-time it looked all over for the Whips as they trailed by two goals. However, the Dons battled back to keep in touch at the top of the group.

TUESDAY 15TH JUNE 1982

Scotland opened their World Cup Finals campaign with a 5-2 win over New Zealand in the Estadio La Rosaleda in Malaga. Aberdeen midfielder Gordon Strachan began the game and former Don Steve Archibald came on as a substitute and scored one of the goals.

WEDNESDAY 16TH JUNE 1937

Eastern Transvaal beat Aberdeen 2-1 in Benoni before an attendance of 5,000 during the Dons' South African tour. This was the club's ninth game in only 22 days.

SATURDAY 16TH JUNE 1990

Former Aberdeen goalkeeper Jim Leighton and Alex McLeish were in the Scotland side that restored pride with an impressive 2-1 win over Sweden in Genoa. The Scots' World Cup hopes were revived after their opening day defeat to Costa Rica.

SUNDAY 17TH JUNE 1956

Aberdeen went down to Everton once during their Canadian tour. On this occasion, a Paddy Buckley goal was all that the Dons had to show in a 3-1 defeat in Toronto. Goals from Harris and Farrel consigned them to their second tour defeat.

MONDAY 18TH JUNE 1956

Aberdeen completed their tour of Canada with a 6-3 defeat against Everton in New York. Bob Wishart and Paddy Buckley scored the goals but it was a tired Dons who had come through their ninth game in less than three weeks. This match had to be re-scheduled as the original meeting was washed out due to heavy rainfall in the New York area.

FRIDAY 18TH JUNE 1982

Willie Miller became the Dons most-capped player – overtaking Bobby Clark's long-standing record of 17 appearances – when he played for Scotland against Brazil in the World Cup in Seville. Gordon Strachan was also in the side and Alex McLeish came on as a substitute in the 4-1 defeat by the Brazilians before a 47,379 crowd.

SATURDAY 19TH JUNE 1937

In what was classed as a Test Match, the Dons played South Africa in Durban as part of their tour in 1937. A crowd of 15,000 turned out to see the tourists win 5-2 with Matt Armstrong scoring three for Aberdeen. The Scots had managed to gradually get used to the hot conditions which were far removed from what they were normally used to.

FRIDAY 19TH JUNE 1964

Former Aberdeen midfielder Brian Grant was born in Bannockburn. Grant was brought to Pittodrie by Alex Ferguson in 1984 in a £40,000 transfer from Stirling Albion. It was not until the arrival of Alex Smith in 1988 that Grant was able to establish himself. In August 1996 a crowd of 9,000 turned out at Pittodrie for his testimonial against Everton. Grant joined Jocky Scott at Hibernian later that year in a £75,000 deal.

WEDNESDAY 20TH JUNE 1934

Graham Leggat, of 1950s' fame, was born in Aberdeen. Leggat started out with Banks O'Dee before joining the Dons in 1953. Graham was in the side that won the League championship and League Cup in 1955. After making his Scotland debut that year, Leggat was seen by many as player of genuine international class. In 1958 he was sold to Fulham for the ridiculously low price of £16,000.

TUESDAY 20TH JUNE 1967

Aberdeen came up against English side Wolverhampton Wanderers in Washington and Jimmy Wilson scored for the Dons in a 1-1 draw. Eddie Turnbull had managed to come over after a spell of sickness. Harry Melrose had been entrusted to take care of the team in his absence and the Wolves game allowed Melrose to make his first appearance of the tour. It emerged after the game that the English side used illegal substitutions during the game and the organisers insisted on the match being replayed at a later date. USA rules stated that only two outfield players could be used while Wolves contrived to send on three.

FRIDAY 21st JUNE 1985

Scotland international Jim Bett joined Aberdeen from Lokeren in a £300,000 transfer. Bett went on to play for the Reds for 10 seasons and also made 25 appearances for his country.

TUESDAY 22nd JUNE 1982

The infamous mix-up between Willie Miller and Alan Hansen resulted in a breakaway goal for the USSR that ended Scotland hopes of qualifying for the latter stages of the World Cup in Spain. Scotland needed the win but a 2-2 draw meant elimination.

TUESDAY 23rd JUNE 1998

Scotland were eliminated from the World Cup in France, going down 3-0 to Morocco in Saint-Etienne. Jim Leighton was the only Aberdeen player in the side although former Don Scott Booth was a late substitution for the Scots.

MONDAY 24th JUNE 1946

Harry Yorston signed for Aberdeen local side St Clements. Brought up in Park Road, near Pittodrie, Yorston went on to become known as the 'Golden Boy' at the club for his style and looks, as much as anything else. He was a prolific scorer for Aberdeen and would go on to be a league and cup winner before shocking the club in 1957 by declaring he was retiring from the game to take up a job as a fish market porter. Yorston later hit the jackpot when he won the football pools in the 1970s.

FRIDAY 25th JUNE 1915

For the first time in the Dons' history, their AGM did not attract sufficient numbers to form a quorum. With the First World War having a devastating effect on resources, the remaining directors assumed sole responsibility for running the club. Rumours persisted that the club were on the verge of withdrawing from the league due to their perilous financial position and the fact that Aberdeen, as an area, was isolated compounded difficulties. Had Aberdeen withdrawn they would certainly have been demoted after the hostilities.

SATURDAY 26TH JUNE 1937

In the second Test Match of the tour, Aberdeen defeated South Africa 5-1 in Johannesburg. However, football was the last thing on the touring party's mind as concern grew for Jackie Benyon who had taken ill six games into the tour. The club were devastated to learn that Jackie died in a Johannesburg hospital that night. Benyon was laid to rest in an emotional ceremony in the South African city. Later, his body was brought back to a permanent resting place in his homeland, Wales.

MONDAY 27TH JUNE 1932

George Thomson joined Aberdeen from Glasgow club St Roch's. Thomson went on to play his part in the great black and gold side of the 1930s and he made 244 appearances for the club, scoring 20 goals before the outbreak of the war in 1939, effectively ended his playing career. Thomson played in the Dons' first Scottish Cup Final in 1937.

WEDNESDAY 28TH JUNE 1967

Frank Munro was on target for Aberdeen as they drew 1-1 with Sunderland in Washington. Harry Melrose set up Jimmy Wilson for the Dons goal. Despite pinning the Wearsiders back for long periods, it was Sunderland that scored against the run of play when Gauden reacted quickly to a Hughes corner that had eluded Bobby Clark.

WEDNESDAY 29TH JUNE 1927

After a hard-fought win over a strong Natal side in Durban, Aberdeen travelled to Pietermaritzburg to face Natal in the second meeting between the sides in four days. The opposition were physically stronger and more agile than the Dons, but they lacked the skill and craft of the tourists. A goal from Benny Yorston could not save Aberdeen from a 2-1 defeat in South Africa.

THURSDAY 30TH JUNE 1927

Jackie Allister was born in Edinburgh. Allister was a £7,500 signing from Chelsea in 1952 and he went on to become part of the famous Aberdeen half-back line that helped the club to a first title in 1955. Allister was a tough, uncompromising defender and was seen as a vital part of that championship side. Capped for Scotland at 'B' level, Allister eventually joined Chesterfield for a £500 fee in 1958.

ABERDEEN FC
On This Day

JULY

SATURDAY 1st JULY 1911

Pat Travers shocked Aberdeen by announcing that he was turning down terms with the club after intimating that he wished to be reinstated as an amateur after Celtic were keen to sign him. That, of course, allowed Travers to sign for any side without any transfer fee and he duly joined the Hoops as an 'amateur' with Aberdeen receiving nothing.

SATURDAY 2nd JULY 1927

As Aberdeen wound down their extensive tour of South Africa, their last big match came against the national Test side in Johannesburg. A double from Benny Yorston was enough to give the Scots a 2-0 win in front of a 30,000 crowd.

MONDAY 3rd JULY 1950

Dave Shaw signed for Aberdeen from Hibernian and was immediately installed as captain. A Scottish international, he went on to manage the Dons for four years after Dave Halliday left for Leicester City in 1955. His last game for the Reds was the 1953 Scottish Cup Final against Rangers. In 1959 he reverted to his trainer role a position he held until 1967.

TUESDAY 4th JULY 1967

Brazilian side Bangu played Aberdeen for the second time in the 1960s when the sides clashed in America in 1967. The Dons gained revenge for their 1-0 defeat in 1961 with a narrow 1-0 win in the Houston Astrodome before a 12,380 attendance. Jimmy Smith was again the Reds scorer with a goal of quality that even the Brazilian opponents admired.

THURSDAY 5th JULY 1906

The AGM at Pittodrie was a lively affair as chairman Harry Wyllie had to fend off probing questions from the Aberdeen shareholders as concern grew as to the quality of the first team. Manager Jimmy Philip was paid £120 for his annual salary while trainer Peter Simpson picked up £83 for his troubles.

WEDNESDAY 5TH JULY 1967

Aberdeen were still in Texas taking part in the Presidents' Cup when news came through that they had been drawn against Icelandic minnows FR Reykjavik in what would be the Dons' first-ever European tie. Reykjavik were the most northerly club in the competition and, although amateurs, they were Icelandic champions at that time.

WEDNESDAY 5TH JULY 1972

The magnificent Maracana in Rio was the venue for Scotland's meeting with Brazil. Aberdeen goalkeeper Bobby Clark was up against some of the best forward players in the world and kept the Brazilians at bay for long spells before he was eventually beaten by a Jairzinho goal on 80 minutes. Also in the Scotland side was former captain Martin Buchan.

WEDNESDAY 6TH JULY 1927

The Dons tour of South Africa came to a close with a 4-1 win over East Rand in Benoni. Aberdeen had completed 14 games in a five-week tour which also included 'Test' matches against South Africa. During the tour Benny Yorston was given his chance to play in the first team and went on to score 17 goals from 13 starts.

WEDNESDAY 7TH JULY 1937

Aberdeen completed their tour of South Africa with an impressive 4-0 win over Western Province in Observatory. A crowd of only 1,000 was present to see Johnny Lang score two of the Dons' four goals.

SATURDAY 8TH JULY 1967

As the Dons closed in on winning their section in the Presidents' Cup in the USA, Irish side Shamrock Rovers shocked Aberdeen with a 2-1 win in Washington. The Reds knew that a win would have taken them through to the final. Despite a second period where the Irish were hit with everything, there was no way through for the Dons. As the Aberdeen players left the field convinced they had blown their chances of progressing, news came through that nearest rivals Stoke City had also lost. There was still hope…

TUESDAY 9TH JULY 2002

After beginning their pre-season with a win at Peterhead, Aberdeen travelled down the coast to face Third Division neighbours Montrose at Links Park. Ebbe Skovdahl was keen to try out some new faces and the Dons won 2-0 with goals from English duo Leon Mike and Ben Thornley.

MONDAY 10TH JULY 1967

Jim Storrie was among the goals as Aberdeen beat Wolverhampton Wanderers 3-0 in Washington as the Dons battled their way through to the Presidents' Cup Final. The game was played under a hostile atmosphere as the English club were ordered to replay the game due to fielding illegal substitutes in the previous match. All the goals came in a nervous second period as the Reds knew that a victory would put them through to face the same Wolves side in the Los Angeles final. The 7,641 Washington DC crowd were off their seats when Jim Storrie put Aberdeen ahead on 55 minutes.

FRIDAY 11TH JULY 1930

Jimmy Philip, the first-ever Aberdeen manager, was tragically killed in a road crash in Belfast. The former Dons boss left his post in 1924 after steering the club through their formative years, and through World War I. Philip was an outspoken manager and was never afraid to champion the Aberdeen cause. He was the driving force behind the club that eventually went through amalgamation and Scottish League status. After leaving his manager's post he became a director at Pittodrie before his untimely passing.

WEDNESDAY 12TH JULY 1905

At the club AGM held at Pittodrie there was great enthusiasm as Aberdeen had been admitted to the First Division for the first time. Chairman Baillie Milne announced that the club had now purchased Pittodrie Park for the sum of £5,668. In all matches that season the team scored 104 goals, conceding 59.

SATURDAY 12TH JULY 2008

Alex Ferguson made an emotional return to Pittodrie with his Manchester United team to help Aberdeen celebrate the 25th anniversary of the Dons' 1983 European Cup Winners' Cup success. Ferguson met up with some of the 'Gothenburg Greats' who made the journey back to Aberdeen for the day. Manchester United won 2-0 with goals in each half from Michael Carrick and Wayne Rooney before a capacity Pittodrie crowd.

SUNDAY 13TH JULY 1952

Former Aberdeen winger Ian Scanlon was born in Birkenshaw. Scanlon was brought to Pittodrie in March 1978 by Billy McNeill after almost giving up the game for good. After being a part of the Notts County side since 1972, he announced that he was to quit as he had lost all interest in football. Scanlon was persuaded to join Aberdeen rather than open a public house in Nottingham and played his part in the Aberdeen side that won the league title in 1980.

FRIDAY 14TH JULY 1967

It was in the LA Coliseum that Aberdeen, as the Washington Whips, played out an epic Presidents' Cup Final against Wolves as their tour of the USA came to a close. A crowd of 17,824 turned out for the final after both Aberdeen (Washington) and Wolverhampton (LA Wolves) had came through their groups to reach the final. The game was a classic that lasted two hours. Apart from some outrageous fouls, Aberdeen had to play for most of the contest without the talented Jimmy Smith, who was sent off for kicking Dave Wagstaffe after the Wolves player had spat on him. Eventually, Aberdeen went down 6-5 in 'overtime' and it was an unfortunate own goal from Ally Shewan that proved decisive. Ron Allen, the Wolves manager, was quick to acknowledge that his team were lucky and had Aberdeen had eleven men on the park for the entire game it would have been a different outcome.

MONDAY 15TH JULY 2002

Darren Young scored against Bran Bergen as Aberdeen continued their preparations for the new season in a 1-1 draw in Norway.

WEDNESDAY 16TH JULY 1952

Jimmy Mitchell signed for Aberdeen after a £10,000 transfer from Morton. The former Queen's Park full-back was capped at league level for Scotland and manager Dave Halliday immediately made Mitchell the Aberdeen captain. He went on to lead the Dons to a first league title in 1955 and was also the Reds captain that lifted the League Cup in October that year. Mitchell went on to make 184 appearances for the club.

SATURDAY 17TH JULY 1943

While the country was in the grip of the war in Europe, a Dons side played St Mirren in a friendly in Paisley. Jock Pattillo was a prolific scorer for Aberdeen during that period and he scored both goals in a 2-1 win over the Paisley side.

FRIDAY 18TH JULY 1975

Ian Hair and Drew Jarvie scored the Aberdeen goals in a 2-1 win over Nuremberg in a pre-season friendly in Germany. Less than 24 hours later, the Dons defeated Bayereuth 2-0 as their tour of Germany came to a close.

FRIDAY 19TH JULY 1996

Russell Anderson signed for Aberdeen from Dyce Boys Club to begin a memorable career at the club. Anderson went on to become captain and made over 300 appearances for the Reds before being awarded a testimonial against Everton in August 2006. The international defender joined Sunderland in 2007 in a £1m transfer and then moved to Plymouth Argyle on loan in February 2008.

TUESDAY 20TH JULY 1971

Aberdeen began their preparations for the new season with a tour to Germany and opened with a 2-0 win over Borussia Dortmund. There were no new signings on show for the Dons as goals from Henning Boel and Joe Harper secured the victory.

SATURDAY 21st JULY 1951

The St Mungo Cup competition was initiated in Glasgow and the leading clubs in Scotland took part. Aberdeen defeated Rangers in the opening round before facing St Mirren at Hampden Park. George Hamilton, Archie Baird and Tommy Bogan scored the Aberdeen goals in a 4-2 win before an 18,000 crowd.

MONDAY 22nd JULY 2003

Aberdeen made the short trip north to face Peterhead at Balmoor as part of their pre-season build-up. New signing Michael Bird scored twice in the Dons' 3-0 win before a 2,000 crowd. Scott Booth was in the Aberdeen side after his return to Pittodrie from Holland.

FRIDAY 23rd JULY 1971

Aberdeen continued their pre-season preparations with a dismal 3-1 defeat against 1860 Munich in Germany. Less than 24 hours later the Dons beat Augsburg 1-0.

THURSDAY 24th JULY 1958

Scotland's most capped keeper, Jim Leighton, was born. He arrived at Pittodrie from Dalry Thistle in 1976. After a spell on loan in the Highland League, Leighton made his debut at Hearts in August 1978. It was not until 1980, however, that he became first choice after Bobby Clark retired. He passed the 500-game mark in his second spell and in 2000 was awarded a testimonial against Middlesbrough.

WEDNESDAY 25th JULY 1951

Aberdeen had reached the semi-final of the St Mungo Cup after defeating St Mirren in the second round. The Dons came up against Hibernian at Celtic Park and a George Hamilton goal helped the Dons to a 1-1 draw. After winning the coin toss to host the replay, a 2-1 win meant a Hampden Park showdown with Celtic.

SATURDAY 26th JULY 1980

Aberdeen opened the season with a Drybrough Cup clash against Airdrie at Pittodrie. It was the first match as champions, and 8,650 turned out. It was also the first game played in front of the new South Terrace cantilever roof. Ian Scanlon scored three in a 4-1 win.

SUNDAY 27TH JULY 2003

Aberdeen won the Bradford City Centenary Trophy after a penalty shoot-out over the home side. The game finished in a disappointing 0-0 draw and the Dons won their first silverware of the season after a 5-4 win before a poor crowd of 2,357.

SATURDAY 28TH JULY 2001

It was a disappointing start to the season as Aberdeen went down 3-0 to Rangers at Pittodrie. The crowd of 18,838 were expecting more from Ebbe Skovdahl's side with Roberto Bisconti making his Dons debut.

SATURDAY 29TH JULY 1972

Holders Aberdeen got their Drybrough Cup defence off to a winning start against St Mirren at Pittodrie. In the opening game of the season, a Joe Harper goal was enough to put the Reds through to a semi-final meeting with Celtic in Glasgow.

WEDNESDAY 30TH JULY 1980

Extra-time was required for Aberdeen to see off a stubborn challenge from Morton in the Dons' Drybrough Cup semi-final at Cappielow. In what was the last season of the competition, two goals from Ian Scanlon helped the Dons through to the final against a side that had proved difficult for Aberdeen in the past. St Mirren were the opposition at Hampden Park.

SATURDAY 31ST JULY 1971

Aberdeen played their first-ever Drybrough Cup tie against East Fife at Bayview. The new sponsored tournament was popular in its infancy and the Dons eased to a 3-0 win with goals from George Buchan, Joe Harper and Arthur Graham.

ABERDEEN FC
On This Day

AUGUST

SATURDAY 1st AUGUST 1891

The Northern League was founded and was competed for by all clubs in the Aberdeen, Tayside and Fife areas. This was the first league that the original Aberdeen FC played in and it flourished in the early years before eventually becoming a secondary competition when the club were admitted to the Scottish League in 1904. The Northern League trophy is still on show in the Pittodrie boardroom.

SATURDAY 1st AUGUST 1992

Duncan Shearer made his debut for the Dons and scored twice in the 3-0 win over Hibernian at Pittodrie. The former Chelsea striker cost Aberdeen £500,000 from Blackburn Rovers. Roy Aitken also made his debut before a 12,503 crowd at Pittodrie as the stadium capacity was cut to 14,000 as the new Richard Donald Stand construction began.

SATURDAY 2nd AUGUST 1941

Germany's Dr Goebbels declared that Britain would never play football again on a Saturday until the Nazis landed and organised it. Aberdeen were among several clubs that was having none of that and in preparation for the hastily organised North Eastern League, the club arranged a trial match at Linksfield. A host of players from other clubs were available including Aberdeen-born Dally Duncan.

WEDNESDAY 2nd AUGUST 1967

Chelsea travelled north to play Aberdeen in a friendly at Pittodrie only two weeks after the club had completed their tour of the USA. Jim Storrie and Jimmy Wilson scored in the Dons' 2-1 win over the Stamford Bridge club.

SATURDAY 2nd AUGUST 1980

The last ever Drybrough Cup competition was won by Aberdeen after a 2-1 win over St Mirren at a sparsely populated Hampden Park. It was 17-year-old Steve Cowan who scored a sensational winner in 74 minutes after Frank McDougall had scored for the Paisley club. Among the crowd of less than 7,000, were Scotland manager Jock Stein and Arsenal boss Don Howe whose side would face Aberdeen at Pittodrie 24 hours later.

SUNDAY 3RD AUGUST 1980

It was Flag Day in Aberdeen as a triumphant Dons squad took their bow in front of 13,768 fans at Pittodrie as the Premier League trophy was presented to captain Willie Miller, and the league flag was also unfurled before the friendly with Arsenal. Aberdeen had defeated St Mirren at Hampden Park the day before to lift the last Drybrough Cup and the Dons continued their winning ways with a 2-1 win over the Gunners. There was also a brief appearance of Clive Allen in an Arsenal shirt after his big money move to Highbury.

SATURDAY 3RD AUGUST 1996

Brian Grant was rewarded for his long service to Aberdeen with a testimonial against Everton at Pittodrie. Grant was signed by Alex Ferguson for £50,000 from Stirling Albion in 1984. Only 9,000 turned out to see the visitors win comfortably, 3-1. Billy Dodds scored the Aberdeen consolation.

SATURDAY 3RD AUGUST 2002

Aberdeen opened their season with a 2-1 win over Hibernian at Easter Road. Chris Clark scored an injury-time winner as almost 3,000 Dons fans followed their side to Edinburgh. Recent signing Eric Deloumeaux made his debut after joining from Coventry City.

WEDNESDAY 4TH AUGUST 1971

Aberdeen beat Airdrie 4-1 at Broomfield in the semi-final of the inaugural Drybrough Cup, they'd face Celtic in the Pittodrie final.

SATURDAY 5TH AUGUST 1978

Pittodrie Stadium became the first all-seated stadium in Britain during the summer of this year. The official opening of the facility was in a friendly match against Tottenham Hotspur. The capacity of the ground was 24,000 as the old South Terrace was now seated.

TUESDAY 5TH AUGUST 2003

Liverpool visited Pittodrie as part of the Dons centenary year and an all-ticket full house of 20,469 looked on as the Premiership side won 5-1. New Australian striker David Zdrilic opened the scoring for the Dons but Michael Owen led the Liverpool response.

SATURDAY 6TH AUGUST 1966

Dave Smith was on the mark for Aberdeen with a penalty that gave his side a 2-1 win over Manchester City at Pittodrie. The Dons kept their long undefeated record at home against English opposition with a hard-fought win before a 12,000 attendance.

SATURDAY 7TH AUGUST 1971

Less than 24 hours after being appointed Aberdeen manager, Jim Bonthrone celebrated his first success with a 2-1 win over Celtic in the Drybrough Cup Final at Pittodrie. The 26,000 crowd were treated to a classic final between the top two sides in Scotland. Joe Harper and Dave Robb scored the goals. Captain Martin Buchan was presented with the trophy in the Main Stand as thousands of supporters gathered on the pitch.

TUESDAY 8TH AUGUST 2006

Russell Anderson was given a testimonial by Aberdeen following ten seasons with the club. Everton provided the opposition and the Goodison Park side won an exciting game 3-2. An 11,500 Pittodrie crowd turned up to honour their skipper. Anderson moved on to Sunderland a year later in a £1m transfer to the English Premier League.

SATURDAY 9TH AUGUST 1980

Aberdeen were not given the opportunity to unfurl their league flag on the opening day of the 1980/81 season as they facing St Mirren at Paisley. Drew Jarvie made sure the champions got the defence of their title off to a winning start by scoring the only goal of the game in the 23rd minute.

SATURDAY 10TH AUGUST 1985

The new family stand at Pittodrie was still being completed as Aberdeen opened the season with a 3-0 win over Hibernian. The Premier League flag was unfurled before the start and new Aberdeen signing Jim Bett finally made the breakthrough in the 69th minute with a superb shot from the edge of the box. Two late goals from Frank McDougall were perhaps tough on Hibernian.

THURSDAY 10TH AUGUST 2000

Robbie Winters had the distinction of scoring Aberdeen's 150th goal in European competition when he opened the scoring against Bohemian at Pittodrie in a preliminary Uefa Cup match. It all went horribly wrong for the Dons as they conceded two late goals against the Irish side. Despite a 1-0 win over in the return, the Dons went out on away goals and became the first Scottish side to lose to Irish opponents in Europe. Aberdeen had qualified on the back of reaching the Scottish Cup Final the previous season.

SATURDAY 11TH AUGUST 1928

Pittodrie patrons were pleasantly surprised walking down the Merkland Road for the opening game of the season against Cowdenbeath. The club had just completed the ornate granite facade that still stands at the King Street end of the stadium. The club had also completed extending the Main Stand the full length of the pitch which was opened in time for the new season. Aberdeen went on to win 4-2 before a 16,000 attendance.

SATURDAY 12TH AUGUST 1933

Matt Armstrong got the Dons' season off to a flier as Aberdeen defeated Ayr United 8-0 at Pittodrie on the opening day. Armstrong scored five goals, his personal best for the club during a distinguished career. Willie Gall made his debut for the Dons as Jackie Benyon scored twice before a 15,000 attendance.

SATURDAY 12TH AUGUST 1939

With political tensions high in Europe, and World War Two on the horizon, the Scottish season began with Aberdeen defeating Celtic 3-1 at Pittodrie before a 35,000 crowd. New Dons signing Charlie Christie scored one of the goals, but it was all to be in vain. After five league games, the authorities postponed the league season with all results null and void, due to the outbreak of war. Christie played in all five matches but with the league being scrapped, he effectively became the Don that never was!

SATURDAY 12TH AUGUST 1967

Alex Ferguson made his first Pittodrie appearance as a Rangers player in the Dons 1-1 draw with the Ibrox side in a League Cup group match before a 36,600 crowd. Jim Storrie scored a late equaliser for Aberdeen.

SATURDAY 12TH AUGUST 1978

Dons legend Jim Leighton made his competitive debut for Aberdeen as they got their first season under Alex Ferguson off to a flier in a 4-1 win against Hearts at Tynecastle. Two second-half goals from Archibald helped the Dons to a comfortable opening day win before 11,500 fans.

THURSDAY 13TH AUGUST 1903

The first statutory meeting of the Aberdeen FC shareholders was presided over by chairman Baillie Milne. The adoption of the directors apart, which showed that 1530 shares had been applied for and that the preliminary expense of the flotation of the club had been paid. Mr James Philip, the team manager, then gave a short summary on the players that had been signed by the club.

SATURDAY 13TH AUGUST 1938

George Hamilton made his Aberdeen debut in the Dons' 2-1 defeat at Partick Thistle in the opening game of the 1938/39 season. Hamilton was a record buy from Queen of the South in a £2,750 transfer. Wilf Adey and Willie Hume were also playing for the stripes for the first time at Firhill.

SATURDAY 13TH AUGUST 1977

Billy McNeill made his first game in charge one to savour as his new Aberdeen side put Rangers to the sword in a 3-1 win at Pittodrie before a 22,000 crowd. McNeill milked the applause from the home support as he made his way to the dugout for the first time. Two goals in two second-half minutes put Aberdeen in command. McNeill enjoyed endearing himself to the Aberdeen support, sporting a red shirt for the occasion.

SATURDAY 13th AUGUST 1988

New signing Theo Snelders made his debut against Dundee at Dens Park before a 12,222 attendance. The £300,000 replacement for Jim Leighton – who was transferred to Manchester United – went on to become a popular goalkeeper at Pittodrie and won both domestic cup winners' medals before joining Rangers in 1996.

SATURDAY 14th AUGUST 1943

With the country gripped by the war effort in Europe, Aberdeen continued to play regionalised football in the North Eastern League. Jock Pattillo was on form for Aberdeen in a remarkable change in fortunes in the second period. The Dons eclipsed Dunfermline Athletic with seven second-half goals after being two goals down at the interval. Pattillo was regular marksman for Aberdeen during the war and he scored three times.

WEDNESDAY 14th AUGUST 1968

Ally Shewan made his 500th appearance for Aberdeen when Dunfermline Athletic visited Pittodrie in the League Cup. Shewan was the Dons captain and his remarkable consistency saw him become the player with most appearances for the club at that time. New Aberdeen signing Jim Forrest, from Preston North End, scored the only goal of the game.

SATURDAY 14th AUGUST 1982

Alex Ferguson was in prophetic mood as he suggested that his side could do well in Europe that season. Although Aberdeen struggled to a 3-3 draw against Dundee in a League Cup tie, Ferguson was delighted with the contribution of Eric Black who scored all three Aberdeen goals. "Once we iron out a few matters in the defence we do have the players that can make an impact in Europe," was Ferguson's post-match reaction.

SATURDAY 14th AUGUST 1993

Kilmarnock returned to the Premier League for the first time in 12 years and opened the season at Pittodrie. A Paul Kane goal was enough to get the Dons' off to a winning start, in the first league game to be played in front of the new Richard Donald Stand at Pittodrie.

SATURDAY 15TH AUGUST 1903

A first-ever outing for Aberdeen as they welcomed Stenhousemuir to Pittodrie for a Northern League fixture. Dons captain Willie MacAulay scored in a 1-1 draw before an 8,000 attendance. After the thorny issue of the amalgamation of Aberdeen, Orion and Victoria United had been resolved, hopes were high that the new Aberdeen FC would make an immediate impact.

SATURDAY 15TH AUGUST 1914

Bert MacLachlan and George Anderson both made their debut for Aberdeen, after their summer arrival from England, against Dundee at Dens Park in the opening league game of a troubled season. Aberdeen won 3-1 in front of 10,000 spectators.

MONDAY 15TH AUGUST 1921

The initial part of the Main Stand at Pittodrie was officially opened as Aberdeen reserves defeated Dundee 4-1 in an East of Scotland league match. A large crowd of 10,000 turned out see the new facility which was to become the main headquarters of the club and replace the dated 'cricket style' pavilion that was brought down from Cattofield in 1899.

WEDNESDAY 15TH AUGUST 1951

Harry Yorston had the distinction of scoring Aberdeen's 100th goal in the League Cup when he netted against Rangers at Ibrox in the 37th minute. The Dons went on to give the Glasgow side the initiative in the group by losing 2-1 before a huge 60,000 attendance.

WEDNESDAY 15TH AUGUST 1955

The Dons original 'Great Dane', Henning Boel, was born in Ikast, Denmark. Boel was spotted by Aberdeen during their tour of the USA in 1967 and signed for the club a year later. He went on to become a cult figure at Pittodrie with his trademark surging runs from his full-back position, endearing him to the Aberdeen support. Boel was also in the side that won the Scottish Cup in 1970 before a knee injury sustained in a Uefa Cup tie in Germany effectively ended his playing career.

SATURDAY 16TH AUGUST 1919

Pittodrie patrons were in for a shock as football resumed after the end of the war. Albion Rovers opened the new football season and admission prices had doubled since before the war started in 1914. The club had lost out financially during this period and at one point were on the verge of bankruptcy. Jock Hutton was also making his debut for the club in the 2-0 win over Rovers before the 9,000 attendance.

SATURDAY 16TH AUGUST 1941

In a North Eastern league meeting at Pittodrie, Aberdeen defeated Leith Athletic 9-0. Several players guested for the Dons during the war and only Johnstone, Cooper, Dunlop, McCall and Taylor were recognised Aberdeen players.

WEDNESDAY 16TH AUGUST 1972

Eddie Turnbull's Hibernian would go on to win the League Cup that year, but were handed out a tough lesson by Aberdeen in the qualifying group. With two teams going through, Hibs 4-1 defeat at Pittodrie was fortunate that it did not harm their long-term prospects. The 21,000 crowd were delighted to see Aberdeen hit Hibernian hard with three goals in 13 minutes. Aberdeen saved the best for last with Joe Harper scoring from near the touchline, some 40 yards out, with his shot deceiving Jim Herriot.

SUNDAY 16TH AUGUST 1981

Willie Miller welcomed Tottenham Hotspur north to Pittodrie for his testimonial match. Spurs had been defeated by Aberdeen in the previous two meetings in 1978 and 1979 but the English side gained revenge of sorts with a 1-0 win. The decisive goal came from a Garry Brooke penalty on 82 minutes. However, it was Tottenham goalkeeper Aleksic that was busy throughout as the Dons passed up several scoring opportunities. A young Eric Black made his first appearance for Aberdeen as Miller was playing his 451st game for the Dons. Spurs brought the FA Cup along with them, which was on show before the game.

SUNDAY 16TH AUGUST 1998

New signing, Craig Hignett from Middlesbrough, was on show as Aberdeen defeated Celtic 3-2 at Pittodrie in a pulsating match that was live on television. Hignett scored for the Dons but the game was remembered for an astonishing own goal by Celtic winger Reggie Blinker who gave his goalkeeper no chance by heading past Gould from the edge of the box.

WEDNESDAY 17TH AUGUST 1983

Martin Buchan welcomed Aberdeen to Old Trafford to play his Manchester United side in his testimonial match. The European Cup Winners' Cup was paraded by the Aberdeen substitutes at half-time before a 28,000 crowd. The Dons fought back from two Frank Stapleton goals to draw 2-2. Buchan had the rare distinction of being captain for both Aberdeen and Manchester United and he also led both sides to respective FA Cup success.

MONDAY 18TH AUGUST 1980

Archie Knox was appointed assistant manager at Aberdeen after Alex Ferguson moved to replace Pat Stanton. Knox had been a player with Dundee United and St Mirren before embarking on a coaching career with his native Forfar Athletic.

WEDNESDAY 18TH AUGUST 1982

Aberdeen began their European Cup Winners' Cup campaign with a resounding 7-0 win over Swiss side Sion at Pittodrie in what was a preliminary tie. The 13,000 crowd were treated to a marvellous show of pace and power from Aberdeen as six different scorers made the return leg and trip to Switzerland a formality.

WEDNESDAY 18TH AUGUST 1993

The new Richard Donald Stand was officially opened by Princess Anne at a ceremony at Pittodrie. Later that evening, the Dons welcomed old rivals Hamburg to commemorate the opening of the £4.5m complex. The stand was named after Aberdeen chairman Richard Donald who had served the club between 1946-1993 as a director and chairman. His first association with the club was as a player in 1921.

SATURDAY 19TH AUGUST 1905

Aberdeen played their first-ever game in the top-flight of Scottish football in a disappointing 1-0 defeat against Partick Thistle at Pittodrie. After gaining admission to the league in the days before automatic promotion and relegation, the Dons new-look side also included a debut for Willie Lennie, the first Aberdeen player to play for Scotland three years later.

SATURDAY 19TH AUGUST 1961

There were farcical conditions for Aberdeen as they travelled to Tannadice to face Dundee United in a League Cup tie. Dons went down 5-3 despite a double from Bobby Cummings. The preparations could have been better; due to work being carried out at a dilapidated Tannadice, the Aberdeen players had to get changed in a sports field two miles away. At half-time they took their break in a works' canteen!

SATURDAY 20TH AUGUST 1904

Falkirk were the first league opponents for Aberdeen when the new 1904/05 season opened at Pittodrie. John Knowles scored the Dons goal in a 2-1 defeat in what was the only season Aberdeen played in the old Second Division of the Scottish League.

SATURDAY 20TH AUGUST 1910

Pat Travers and Willie Lennie both made their first-team debuts for the club against Raith Rovers in the opening league game of the season. Lennie also scored as Aberdeen defeated the Kirkcaldy side 2-0 before a 7,000 attendance. Travers went on to manage the Dons between 1924 and 1937.

WEDNESDAY 20TH AUGUST 1924

The legendary Alec Jackson made his first appearance for Aberdeen in a friendly against Elgin City at Pittodrie. Jackson would go on to become one of the Scottish heroes in the 1928 international against England at Wembley, scoring three in the 5-1 win. His Aberdeen career got off to a less auspicious start in a low-key 2-1 win over the Highland League side in what was the first game at Pittodrie that season, played in front of 6,000 fans.

SATURDAY 21st AUGUST 1965

Rangers travelled to Pittodrie for a League Cup tie that offered the Dons an opportunity to build on their opening two group wins. Young Tom McMillan was drafted into the side and he put the shackles on Rangers' Jim Forrest as Aberdeen took full advantage when opposing goalkeeper Martin was withdrawn with concussion. Davie Wilson went in goal but he could not prevent the Dons hitting Rangers with two late goals from Ravn and Little.

TUESDAY 22nd AUGUST 1899

The last Aberdeen game played at the Chanonry in Old Aberdeen, before the club moved to their new home at Pittodrie, was a 2-1 defeat to fierce local rivals Orion in a friendly match that attracted a 3,000 crowd.

MONDAY 22nd AUGUST 1910

Third Lanark held Aberdeen in a 2-2 draw in what was the Dons' second league game of the 1910/11 season. Hopes were high at Pittodrie that a challenge for the league could be made by the best Aberdeen side assembled in their short history. Jimmy Soye and Angus McIntosh scored for the visitors before a 6,000 crowd at Cathkin Park.

SATURDAY 22nd AUGUST 1970

Joe Harper completed a personal triumph with four goals in the Dons 7-3 defeat of Airdrie in a League Cup tie. Harper showed all his class as the Reds raced into a 5-1 lead by the interval. Drew Jarvie, who would later join Aberdeen, managed to score for Airdrie before two late Dons goals.

TUESDAY 22nd AUGUST 2006

It was humiliation for Aberdeen as they were knocked out of the League Cup by lowly Queen's Park. Despite dominating their amateur opponents throughout the game – and in the extra time period – the Dons could not make the breakthrough and paid a heavy price by going down 5-3 on penalties. The game was switched from Hampden Park to Firhill where conditions were better suited to the Glasgow club.

SATURDAY 23RD AUGUST 1924

Alex Jackson made his Aberdeen debut in a 1-0 defeat at home to Rangers before an 18,000 crowd. Jackson was not the only new face on show that day as namesake Walter also made his debut for the Dons. To confuse matters further, Aberdeen had no less than four 'Jacksons' on their books that season and Alex and Walter were joined by WK and Jimmy in the first team.

TUESDAY 23RD AUGUST 1994

Gothenburg seemed an age away as Aberdeen were humiliated in the preliminary round of the Uefa Cup against Latvian side Skonto Riga. Following an acceptable, but uninspiring, 0-0 draw in Riga, the Dons could not break down the Latvians in the Pittodrie return. Paul Kane's last minute goal meant that the 1-1 draw put Aberdeen out on away goals.

WEDNESDAY 24TH AUGUST 1983

Aberdeen opened the new season with a comfortable 9-0 win over Raith Rovers in the League Cup. While Raith may have been languishing in the lower leagues, they were simply outclassed by an Aberdeen side that were looking to retain the league championship for the first time. Eric Black helped himself to four goals while Billy Stark announced his arrival to the side with a hat-trick. The return in Kirkcaldy three days later resulted in a 3-0 win for the Dons.

SATURDAY 25TH AUGUST 1945

Stan Williams stamped his class all over Pittodrie for the visit of St Mirren. It was the first season of football in the immediate aftermath of the war and South African-born Williams led the way with three of the Dons' six goals in the 6-1 win in the Southern league Division 'A' fixture. Alex Dyer, who had guested for Aberdeen during the war, was also among the goals in front of 12,000 Pittodrie supporters.

WEDNESDAY 26TH AUGUST 1992

Duncan Shearer scored three as Aberdeen swept aside the Falkirk challenge in a convincing 4-1 win at Brockville – with 8,022 in attendance – to make progress through to the semi-final of the League Cup. Brian Irvine was also on target against his former club.

SATURDAY 26TH AUGUST 1995

Aberdeen opened their league campaign at the same venue where they had to fight for their lives two months earlier. The Dons' 3-2 win over Falkirk at Brockville suggested that they had put their troubles behind them. With no new players on show, it was the same squad that Reds boss Roy Aitken pinned his faith on. Billy Dodds was one of the Aberdeen scorers before a 6,647 crowd.

WEDNESDAY 27TH AUGUST 1919

Long-serving Aberdeen utility player Bobby Hannah was rewarded for his loyal service to the Dons with a testimonial match against Dundee at Pittodrie. More than 6,000 turned out to see Aberdeen hold their opposition to a 2-2 draw.

WEDNESDAY 27TH AUGUST 1969

With goal difference involved, the Dons knew that even a one-goal defeat at Hibernian would be enough to take them through to the latter stages of the League Cup. The Aberdeen defence had a far more resolute look about it and the Dons were well worth their 0-0 draw. The result meant they finished top of their section with eight points.

WEDNESDAY 27TH AUGUST 1980

The home and away format of the League Cup brought Berwick Rangers to Pittodrie for what turned out to be an easy win for the Dons. The 8-1 victory made a mockery of the second leg. The 7,571 attendance took the chance to pay tribute to goalkeeper Bobby Clark who was presented with an award from Rothmans before the game for his services to football. He joined David Johnson of Liverpool and John Robertson of Nottingham Forest in receiving recognition.

SATURDAY 28TH AUGUST 1965

One of Eddie Turnbull's first transfers was to take Queen's Park goalkeeper Bobby Clark to Pittodrie. Clark made his debut against Clyde in a 2-0 win at Pittodrie in a League Cup group match before a 12,000 attendance. Clark went on to establish himself in the side that season.

WEDNESDAY 28TH AUGUST 1985

When Aberdeen won the League Cup in 1985 they went through each round without conceding a single goal. In the third round tie against St Johnstone at their old Muirton Park ground, goals from John Hewitt and Frank McDougall put Aberdeen through to face Hearts in the quarter-final. Young midfielder Steve Gray made his debut for the Dons before a 5,100 crowd in Perth.

SATURDAY 29TH AUGUST 1903

The first season of Aberdeen Football Club was mainly focused on their involvement in the Northern League. Expectations were high that the Dons would do well enough in the regional league, which would ultimately help their cause to gain admission to the Scottish League. St Johnstone were no match for Aberdeen, losing 5-1 with Dave Mackay scoring twice.

SATURDAY 29TH AUGUST 1908

Aberdeen had travel problems on their way to play Clyde in Glasgow. The Dons went down 2-1 at Shawfield before a 10,000 attendance. The train journey south was fraught with delays and it took the Aberdeen party almost five hours to complete.

SATURDAY 29TH AUGUST 1936

Frank Dunlop made his debut for Aberdeen in the 4-0 win over Falkirk at Pittodrie. Dunlop joined the Dons along with goalkeeper George Johnstone from the successful Benburb Junior side earlier that year. Dunlop had the distinction of becoming the first Aberdeen player to lift the Scottish Cup in 1947 and emigrated to South Africa in 1948 after playing 146 games for the Dons in a career that was cut short by the war in Europe.

WEDNESDAY 29TH AUGUST 1951

In the days before floodlights at Pittodrie, rivals Rangers flew to Aberdeen for a midweek League Cup tie. It was the legendary Jimmy Delaney in the twilight of his career that scored for Aberdeen in a 2-1 win before a 28,000 crowd. The game began at 5.30pm to make sure it would be finished in reasonable light.

WEDNESDAY 29TH AUGUST 1956

Aberdeen won their first game of the season with a convincing 4-1 victory over East Fife at Pittodrie in the League Cup. Graham Leggat scored two and the 17,000 crowd were relieved the Dons had finally managed to win. With Rangers and Celtic in the Dons qualifying group, it was a tough start to the 1956/57 campaign.

SATURDAY 30TH AUGUST 1975

A new era for Scottish football as the first-ever Premier League matches were played. Aberdeen had the misfortune to concede the first goal scored when Dundee's Bobby Ford netted in two minutes as Aberdeen lost 3-2 at Dens Park before a 6,050 crowd.

SATURDAY 30TH AUGUST 1980

The story of a foreign goalkeeper making his debut in England and scoring for Aberdeen! The Dons completed the formality of beating Berwick Rangers in the League Cup, but the game was remembered for an astonishing goal from Aberdeen debutant Marc de Clerck. The Belgian keeper was making his first Reds appearance and his huge clearance bounced once and over Berwick goalkeeper Davidson and into the goal. The Dons won 4-0, completing a 12-1 aggregate victory.

SUNDAY 31ST AUGUST 1980

Joe Harper was rewarded with a testimonial against an International Select XI in front of 13,500 fans at Pittodrie. Harper took his bow in front of the Aberdeen support on crutches as he was recovering from a knee injury. Jim Leighton scored his one and only goal for the club when he converted a penalty as the game ended in an 8-6 win for Aberdeen.

ABERDEEN FC
On This Day

SEPTEMBER

FRIDAY 1st SEPTEMBER 1899

Pittodrie was a busy place as the finishing touches were being put to the new ground which was due to open against Dumbarton. Club officials were running the rule over the works that were completed in time. The new playing surface was completed and the 130 x 70 yard ground was a scene of several green-keepers painstakingly tending to the new pitch. The capacity was set at 10,000 with plans to increase it to 32,000.

WEDNESDAY 1st SEPTEMBER 1982

The beautiful surroundings of the Swiss Alpine region did not detract from the Dons' fluent style that completed the formality of seeing off Sion in the European Cup Winners' Cup. The 4-1 win in Switzerland followed the Reds' 7-0 home win, prompting the Sion coach to claim that the Aberdeen players "were from another planet". A rare goal from Willie Miller was the highlight of a game that the Scottish side simply strolled through.

SATURDAY 2nd SEPTEMBER 1899

Pittodrie was officially opened when Aberdeen welcomed Dumbarton to mark the occasion. Alex Shiach was the Aberdeen hero as he scored the first-ever goal at the ground as the home side ran out easy 7-1 winners. The new stadium had a 10,000 capacity with a small grandstand built in time for the opening match. The changing facilities still left a lot to be desired; players had to change in a nearby house, while hot water was still a luxury.

SATURDAY 2nd SEPTEMBER 1939

A makeshift Aberdeen side were well beaten by St Johnstone in the Dons' fifth league game of the season. Political unrest across Europe was in everyone's thoughts at that time. A day later war was declared in Europe and all competitions were declared null and void.

WEDNESDAY 2ND SEPTEMBER 1964

The Summer Cup Final from the previous season was held over until Autumn, and finally played at Pittodrie with Hibernian emerging as 3-1 winners. Ernie Winchester scored the only Aberdeen goal in a disappointing outcome for the Dons who had scorned chances in the previous two meetings.

SATURDAY 2ND SEPTEMBER 1967

Controversy at Pittodrie as Celtic defeated Aberdeen 5-1 in the League Cup. Referee JRP Gordon was attacked by a man and his dog, no less, as he awarded Celtic a penalty after Lennox had hurdled Bobby Clark. Worse was to follow for Aberdeen as Gordon ordered Gemmell's penalty to be taken again after Clark saved.

SUNDAY 3RD SEPTEMBER 1978

A full house of 24,000 filled Pittodrie to pay tribute to goalkeeper Bobby Clark who was enjoying his testimonial year with Aberdeen. Clark had joined Aberdeen in 1965 and he became the Dons most capped player during his career, and also picked up a complete set of domestic winners medals at Pittodrie. A Former Dons XI won 1-0 as many former players and managers returned for the day.

WEDNESDAY 3RD SEPTEMBER 1980

Controversy at Ibrox as the bad feeling between the clubs continued after Rangers explosive League Cup clash at Ibrox. With John McMaster on the ground injured, Rangers winger Johnston stamped on the Dons player's neck which required immediate attention from the Aberdeen physio.

SATURDAY 3RD SEPTEMBER 1983

Aberdeen welcomed newly promoted St Johnstone back to the Premier League for the first time since 1976 with a 5-0 defeat that posted the club's intent to take the title that year. After their stunning European Cup Winners' Cup success, manager Ferguson targeted the league as his top priority. It was not to be a happy return for the Perth side as they would face Aberdeen six times that season; losing every game and failing to register a goal.

TUESDAY 3rd SEPTEMBER 1996

Dean Windass and Billy Dodds were the Aberdeen scorers in a remarkable League Cup tie against Morton at Cappielow. The visitors won a sensational game 7-3 with Windass scoring four – and Dodds three – as the Dons ran riot in an extra-time period after the teams had finished level after 90 minutes.

SATURDAY 4th SEPTEMBER 1976

Aberdeen opened their league campaign and were a goal behind after only 20 seconds when Drew Busby beat Bobby Clark from close range. Joe Harper helped restore parity when he set up Ian Fleming, before Dave Robb seemed to have given Aberdeen victory with four minutes left. A late slip allowed a shot for Park to squeeze over the line to earn Hearts a draw they barely deserved.

SATURDAY 5th SEPTEMBER 1964

Despite a promising start to the season against St Mirren, the Dons came off the rails against a Dundee side at Dens Park that never looked like losing after Andy Penman put the home side ahead in 16 minutes. A young Jocky Scott from Aberdeen was making his first appearances for Dundee and the 16-year-old had enough guile to deceive Doug Coutts into gaining an early penalty. Ernie Winchester scored a late consolation for Aberdeen.

WEDNESDAY 6th SEPTEMBER 1939

The Scottish League announced that all competitive football would cease immediately as Britain declared war on Germany. All player contracts were suspended and the league programme was stopped immediately with all results becoming void.

WEDNESDAY 6th SEPTEMBER 1967

European football arrived at Pittodrie for the first time when Icelandic amateurs KR Reykjavik were beaten 10-0 in a European Cup Winners' Cup first round tie. Aberdeen were expected to be too strong and that proved to be the case as Frank Munro scored a hat-trick before a 14,000 crowd. Home keeper Bobby Clark was a spectator throughout and his only involvement was dealing with an occasional back pass from a team-mate.

SATURDAY 7TH SEPTEMBER 1929

The attendance record at Pittodrie was broken for the visit of Rangers when 32,000 filled the ground. It was the exact capacity and it was reported that many missed out, taking up a vantage point at the nearby 'Misers Hilly,' the one area outside of Pittodrie that offered a free view of the action. Alex Cheyne scored for Aberdeen in the 1-1 draw against Rangers.

SUNDAY 7TH SEPTEMBER 1997

The SFA were heavily criticised in the build-up to the visit of Belarus to Pittodrie in 1997. As the nation was coming to terms with the loss of Princess Diana, the game was eventually put back 24 hours to allow the nation to grieve on the day of the funeral. Scotland eventually defeated Belarus 4-1 with Kevin Gallacher and David Hopkin scoring two goals apiece. The Scots remained in contention to qualify for the 1998 World Cup in front of a 20,160 crowd.

SATURDAY 8TH SEPTEMBER 1951

The legendary Jimmy Delaney scored the Dons' third goal in a 3-0 victory over St Mirren as Aberdeen opened their league season with a win. However, there was plenty of controversy 12 minutes from time when the Dons' Pat McKenna came to blows with Saints' Burrell. Both were sent off and McKenna was later suspended for 21 days.

WEDNESDAY 8TH SEPTEMBER 1993

Scotland played Switzerland in a World Cup qualifier at Pittodrie, with John Collins scoring in the 1-1 draw before a capacity 21,500 crowd. After the game, Scotland coach Andy Roxburgh announced he was stepping down after seven years in charge. Scott Booth, Stewart McKimmie, Brian Irvine and sub Eoin Jess were the Aberdeen players on international duty.

SATURDAY 9TH SEPTEMBER 1967

The Dons opened their league campaign at home to Dundee with a 4-2 win over their Angus neighbours. Following a tough League Cup section, Aberdeen had played their first-ever European tie three days earlier. The 14,000 crowd were impressed with young local lad Ian Taylor as he scored twice to end Dundee's long unbeaten run.

MONDAY 10TH SEPTEMBER 1906

The first-ever League Flag was unfurled at Pittodrie during the interval in an East of Scotland fixture against Falkirk. Aberdeen celebrated in style with a 6-1 win after Harry Wyllie, the club chairman, hoisted the flag which marked the winning of the Northern League and the East of Scotland titles.

SATURDAY 10TH SEPTEMBER 1927

Aberdeen defeated Hibernian 4-2 at Pittodrie with Scotland international Alex Cheyne in sensational form. The inside-forward, renowned for scoring direct from corner kicks, scored three of the Dons four goals in 10 minutes against the Easter Road side before a 12,000 crowd.

SATURDAY 10TH SEPTEMBER 1955

League champions Aberdeen began their defence of the championship with a resounding 6-2 win over Hibernian at Pittodrie. The home side had been disappointed that Hibs had been put forward by the SFA to represent Scotland in the new European Cup. As champions, Aberdeen expected that honour. Paddy Buckley put the Edinburgh side to the sword with three goals before a 17,000 attendance.

MONDAY 10TH SEPTEMBER 1962

Scotland international George Mulhall was sold to Sunderland in a £23,000 deal. Mulhall joined Aberdeen in 1953 but had to bide his time before making the first team at Pittodrie. In 1969 he moved to South Africa and after two years returned to British football to take up various coaching roles.

SATURDAY 11TH SEPTEMBER 1954

A fantastic start to the new season as the Dons opened their league campaign with a resounding 5-0 win over Stirling Albion. It was the beginning of a successful league title challenge.

SATURDAY 12TH SEPTEMBER 1964

After an hour of the Dons game against St Johnstone, Aberdeen had cruised into a commanding 5-2 lead. With Doug Coutts in an unfamiliar wide role, the Reds somehow capitulated and allowed the visitors to claw back three goals, the last of which came in the final minute from Richmond to level the game at 5-5.

SATURDAY 13TH SEPTEMBER 1947

Queen of the South were shown no mercy by an Aberdeen side that took full advantage of their opponent's injury problems. The Dons went into this final group game of their League Cup section needing a barrow load of goals to see off the challenge from Motherwell. They were helped along the way as the visitors were eventually reduced to nine men that included a stand-in goalkeeper. The second half was played entirely in front of the visitors' goal and Aberdeen hit eight goals in the second period to win the tie 9-0 and, incredibly, through to the latter stages.

WEDNESDAY 13TH SEPTEMBER 1967

A first away tie in Europe for Aberdeen concluded the formality of disposing of Icelandic side Reykjavik. The Dons 4-1 win in the Municipal Stadium completed an aggregate 14-1 rout. Jim Kirkland was a surprise debutant for the visitors. The Dons eased up after going four goals ahead and the 1,500 crowd had to wait until the 74th minute when Hafsteinsson scored with a fine volley, the only occasion that Bobby Clark was beaten over the two legs.

WEDNESDAY 13TH SEPTEMBER 1972

Aberdeen lost their first-ever game in European competition when German side Borussia Monchengladbach won 3-2 in a first round Uefa Cup tie. Günter Netzer was in imperious form for the visitors dominating the midfield to give the slick Germans a vital lead. The Dons came storming back in the second half, coming back from two goals down to level the game. However, a late goal from Jensen handed Aberdeen a first home defeat in Europe.

SATURDAY 13TH SEPTEMBER 1975

Controversy at Pittodrie as defender Willie Young tore off his shirt and threw it at the Aberdeen dugout after being substituted in the Dons 3-1 defeat at home to Dundee United. It signalled the end for Young as he was soon sold to Tottenham Hotspur in a £125,000 deal.

WEDNESDAY 14TH SEPTEMBER 1932

Ireland international Paddy Moore scored a record six goals in the Dons 8-2 win over Falkirk at Pittodrie. Moore was signed from Shamrock Rovers in May 1932, as a replacement for Benny Yorston, and was in a rich vein of form scoring in ten consecutive matches for Aberdeen. Moore also scored three goals for Ireland in a 4-3 win over Belgium in 1934 and played in 74 matches for Aberdeen – scoring 47 goals – before returning to Shamrock Rovers in 1935.

WEDNESDAY 14TH SEPTEMBER 1977

Belgian club RWD Molenbeek were the Dons first round opponents in the 1977 Uefa Cup. Aberdeen came up against a side that had reached the last four of the competition a year previously, and the 0-0 draw in the away leg suggested that they could finish the job at Pittodrie.

WEDNESDAY 14TH SEPTEMBER 1983

Aberdeen opened the defence of their European Cup Winners' Cup in Iceland against local champions Akranes. The 5,500 crowd were ecstatic when Halldorsson put Akranes ahead. However, Mark McGhee levelled immediately and his second goal two minutes from time eased the holders through.

TUESDAY 14TH SEPTEMBER 1993

The lowest-ever attendance for an Aberdeen European tie was created when only 656 turned up to the Dons' European Cup Winners' Cup tie against Valur in Reykjavik. Aberdeen eased through in a 3-0 win with Eoin Jess scoring twice. The Dons won the second leg 4-0 to set up a meeting with Italian side Torino.

SATURDAY 15TH SEPTEMBER 1951

Two goals in the final seven minutes secured a point for Aberdeen in an astonishing game against Hibernian. The 30,000 Easter Road crowd were treated to a classic as the home side looked out of sight as they went in at the interval 4-1 ahead. To add to Dons woes, Alec Young was carried off early in the second half. The ten men launched an incredible comeback and Tommy Lowrie levelled from a corner in the last minute.

SATURDAY 15TH SEPTEMBER 1962

Dunfermline arrived at Pittodrie having scored ten goals in their previous two matches. Charlie Cooke then set about tormenting the Pars defence as the Dons won 4-0, with both Cooke and Winchester scoring two goals each. Cooke had been attracting the attention of scouts from English sides all season, and following his latest display against Dunfermline, rumours persisted that he would be sold.

WEDNESDAY 15TH SEPTEMBER 1971

Celta Vigo provided the opposition for the Dons first-ever Uefa Cup tie in Spain. It was also a European baptism for Celta and goals from Joe Harper and Jim Forrest gave Aberdeen a first leg lead to take back to Pittodrie. In front of a passionate 30,000 crowd, the Reds faced a side that had gone unbeaten at home for more than a year, in what was one of the Dons' finest performances on foreign soil.

WEDNESDAY 15TH SEPTEMBER 1982

John Hewitt scored the only goal of the game as Aberdeen took a slender advantage to Tirana for the return leg of their European Cup Winners' Cup tie against the Albanians. Alex Ferguson was disappointed not to have seen the opposition before the first game. Tirana were certainly an unknown quantity, but Aberdeen only had themselves to blame for not adding to their first leg advantage, after a succession of missed chances in the second period.

SATURDAY 16TH SEPTEMBER 1911

Pittodrie was closed for two weeks by the SFA following crowd trouble during the visit of Rangers. Aberdeen had gone down 2-1 against the Ibrox club amid controversial scenes as the home side were given a tough time by the officials. That dissention spread to the terraces and the visiting players were subjected to a barrage of stones as they left the field.

SATURDAY 16TH SEPTEMBER 1950

A marathon League Cup tie against Hibernian began with Aberdeen taking a 4-1 first leg lead before a huge 42,000 Pittodrie crowd. Despite going a goal behind through Johnstone, the Dons came storming back to take command of the tie and a seemingly unassailable lead. A similar defeat in the Easter Road return meant a third game at Ibrox, which was also drawn. In the days before penalty shoot-outs, a fourth game in 17 days at Hampden Park was required; Aberdeen ran out of steam and went down 5-1.

SATURDAY 16TH SEPTEMBER 1961

Lewis Thom, the 17-year-old winger, made his debut for the Dons as Dundee were beaten 3-1 at Pittodrie. The 12,000 crowd were surprised to see a linesman flag for hand ball when Dundee defender Hamilton headed the ball off the line. George Kinnell made no mistake from the resultant penalty kick as Aberdeen took full advantage of the poor decision.

WEDNESDAY 16TH SEPTEMBER 1970

A classic European night at Pittodrie as hopes were high that Aberdeen could make an impact in the European arena after winning the Scottish Cup. Hungarian side Honved visited Pittodrie in the opening round of the European Cup Winners' Cup and the Dons managed to take a 3-1 lead with them for the return leg. Goals from Joe Harper, Arthur Graham and Steve Murray kept the 21,455 crowd happy. Aberdeen had to fight back from a goal down after Bobby Clark had turned Kocsis' header on to the post for Pusztai to pounce.

SATURDAY 16TH SEPTEMBER 1978

A last-minute Dom Sullivan goal gave Aberdeen a 1-1 draw against Rangers at Ibrox, prompting the infamous approach by new manager Ferguson who was seething that his players were delighted to only draw in Glasgow. Within weeks changes were made by Ferguson as he began to build his Pittodrie dynasty.

WEDNESDAY 16TH SEPTEMBER 1981

John Hewitt scored the Dons goal as Aberdeen held Uefa Cup holders Ipswich at Portman Road in a 1-1 draw. The almost cynical English press were even impressed by an Scottish side that showed real quality and were unlucky not to take a lead back to Pittodrie.

SATURDAY 17TH SEPTEMBER 1910

Joy for Aberdeen as they registered a first-ever win over Rangers. The Dons had shown their title challenge was serious by inflicting a 4-2 defeat at Ibrox against the league leaders. Tom Murray and Willie Lennie were among the goals as Aberdeen drew level with Rangers at the summit. The 17,000 Ibrox crowd were stunned. The Dons remained undefeated that season.

TUESDAY 17TH SEPTEMBER 1968

Political unrest in Eastern Europe meant that the draw for the Inter Cities Fairs Cup was regionalised, much to Aberdeen's dismay. The Dons were drawn against Bulgarian side Slavia Sofia. A first-ever trip behind the Iron Curtain prompted the Reds to adopt a defensive approach which neither the Bulgarians, or the searing heat, could break down in a 0-0 draw.

WEDNESDAY 17TH SEPTEMBER 1980

European Champions Cup football came to town for the first time as Aberdeen welcomed Austrian champions Memphis to Pittodrie for the Dons' first-ever European Cup-tie. Mark McGhee made history for the Dons, scoring the only goal of the game on 31 minutes. The visitors had high hopes of making an impact in Europe that year; led by the impressive Walter Schachner, the Austrians came up against an Aberdeen defence that stood firm.

TUESDAY 17th SEPTEMBER 2002

Hertha Berlin visited Pittodrie in the first round of the Uefa Cup. The game marked the Dons' 100th in European football – a journey that began in 1967. The Germans held Aberdeen to a 0-0 draw before edging the Dons out in the Olympic Stadium return.

WEDNESDAY 18th SEPTEMBER 1991

Danish side BK1903 from Copenhagen shocked Aberdeen in their Uefa Cup tie with a 1-0 win at Pittodrie. Jocky Scott resigned as co-manager in the aftermath as the Dons went out of Europe in the first round. The result sparked protests from a section of the support outside the stadium after the game.

WEDNESDAY 19th SEPTEMBER 1973

Irish part-time side Finn Harps made their European debut against Aberdeen at Pittodrie before a 10,700 attendance. The Reds took a 4-1 lead to Ireland in the opening round of the Uefa Cup. Drew Jarvie scored twice as the Dons could have threatened their European scoring record, such was their dominance.

WEDNESDAY 19th SEPTEMBER 1979

German side Eintracht Frankfurt were famed for their involvement in the 1960 European Cup Final and they were the Dons' opponents in this Uefa Cup encounter. Frankfurt had six German internationals in their side, but it was South Korean Cha Bum Kum that caught the eye. He scored the opening goal before Joe Harper showed his class as he beat two defenders to level for the Dons before the 20,000 crowd.

WEDNESDAY 19th SEPTEMBER 1984

As one of the top seeds in the European Champions Cup, Aberdeen could have expected an easier draw than Berlin from East Germany in the opening round. Two Eric Black goals in the first leg at Pittodrie seemed to set Aberdeen on their way. However, the Germans scored a vital away goal in 82 minutes when Schulz was left unmarked in the box to head past Jim Leighton.

SATURDAY 20TH SEPTEMBER 1969

Strange times at Pittodrie as international goalkeeper Bobby Clark starts against St Johnstone in Perth... at centre-half! Clark was described as the best header of the ball at the club but manager Turnbull was not impressed after Aberdeen went down 3-1. Clark's deputy was Ernie McGarr, who would play for Scotland against Ireland in Dublin 24 hours later.

WEDNESDAY 20TH SEPTEMBER 1972

A good day at the office for Aberdeen as they announced the signing of Hungarian international Zoltan Varga from Hertha Berlin in a £40,000 deal. The deal came about after Dons boss Jim Bonthrone made initial enquiries when Monchengladbach were at Pittodrie on Uefa Cup duty. Later that evening Varga was in the stands to see Aberdeen hit an incredible eight second-half goals to defeat Falkirk 8-0 in a League Cup tie.

TUESDAY 20TH SEPTEMBER 1988

Goals from John Hewitt and Davie Dodds sent Aberdeen through to the League Cup Final after a 2-0 win over Dundee United at Dens Park. The Aberdeen support made up the bulk of the 18,491 crowd and after Hewitt opened his account on two minutes the Dons controlled the match as United were forced to abandon their defensive tactics.

WEDNESDAY 20TH SEPTEMBER 1989

Ian Cameron scored the goal that took Aberdeen through to the League Cup Final after a 1-0 win over Celtic at Hampden Park. The Reds were going for a third final in succession after beating Albion Rovers, Airdrie and St Mirren to reach the last four.

WEDNESDAY 21ST SEPTEMBER 1921

Harry Blackwell made his Aberdeen debut against Clydebank in a 1-1 draw after joining from Scunthorpe United. The experienced goalkeeper went on to become a popular figure at Pittodrie and he was well known to be unorthodox. In the Dons record 13-0 win over Peterhead in 1923, Blackwell adorned a raincoat and took shelter under an umbrella during the game as all the action was at the other end!

SATURDAY 21st SEPTEMBER 1946

George Hamilton scored the Dons first-ever goal in the League Cup as Aberdeen defeated Falkirk 4-3 in their League Cup group match. Hamilton scored all four Dons goals before a 25,000 crowd. All four Hamilton efforts came in a frantic 25-minute spell in the first half.

WEDNESDAY 21st SEPTEMBER 1966

Progress was made in the League Cup by Aberdeen after a 3-0 victory over Morton put the Dons through to the last four in a 4-3 aggregate win. The Dons trailed 3-1 from the first leg. With five minutes left, the Reds were one goal ahead and out of the cup. Jimmy Smith then looked to have taken the game into extra time before Jens Petersen scored with a superb goal in the final minute. The 30,000 crowd were in raptures.

SATURDAY 22nd SEPTEMBER 1984

Dumbarton boss Davie Wilson claimed that when Aberdeen "Play like that, and with that system, they are unbeatable," after the Dons 2-0 win at newly-promoted Dumbarton. Aberdeen had adopted a new three-man defensive system with Cooper, McLeish and Miller and there seemed no way through for opponents. This was the Reds' seventh league game of the season and with only one point dropped, they were clear favourites to retain the championship.

SATURDAY 23rd SEPTEMBER 1961

Airdrie gave Aberdeen a harsh lesson as they hammered the Dons 7-1 in what was one of the darkest days for the club under Tommy Pearson. The result was a real shock as the Dons defence totally crumbled against a side that had not won, or gained a single point, before the clash at Broomfield.

WEDNESDAY 24th SEPTEMBER 1969

After a 0-0 draw at Pittodrie in the first leg, Aberdeen were under pressure in their League Cup quarter-final return match against Celtic at Parkhead. Jim Forrest shocked the bulk of the 47,000 crowd by scoring in 31 minutes as the Dons looked to hold on. Two goals in three second-half minutes ended Aberdeen hopes.

WEDNESDAY 24TH SEPTEMBER 1980

It was quick revenge for Aberdeen as they defeated Rangers 3-1 in the second leg of their League Cup tie. Trailing 1-0 from the first game at Ibrox, Aberdeen set about retrieving the tie. John McMaster levelled after five minutes with a superb shot from the edge of the box. By the time Forsyth pole-axed John Hewitt in the final minute it was all over and Strachan completed the win from the penalty spot.

SATURDAY 25TH SEPTEMBER 1971

Despite losing manager Eddie Turnbull to Hibernian on the eve of the season, Aberdeen had made an impressive start to the season under Jim Bonthrone. After winning the inaugural Drybrough Cup the Dons made progress in the Uefa Cup after beating Celta Vigo and they continued their fine form with a 2-0 win over Rangers at Ibrox. By the time Joe Harper hit a superb volley past McCloy on 78 minutes, the vast majority of the 41,236 Glasgow crowd had deserted the stands.

THURSDAY 26TH SEPTEMBER 1945

Bobby Clark, the Dons most-capped player of the 1970s was born in Glasgow. Clark was one of Eddie Turnbull's first signings in 1965 from Queen's Park and went on to become the Dons number one goalkeeper until his retirement in 1980. In between times he won a full set of domestic winners' medals and was capped 17 times for Scotland; a club record at the time. Bobby remains involved in the game to the present day, coaching the successful Notre Dame sides in the USA.

TUESDAY 26TH SEPTEMBER 1950

Manchester United's stay in Aberdeen for the traditional holiday fixture was longer than expected as the original friendly meeting was postponed due to the heavy rain and waterlogged pitch. A day later, the sides met at Pittodrie and an exciting friendly ended in a high-scoring 5-3 win for the visitors.

THURSDAY 27th SEPTEMBER 1906

It was success for Aberdeen as they won the McCrae Cup, the trophy that went with winning the East of Scotland League. The Dons defeated Hearts 2-0 at Pittodrie before an 8,000 crowd. Goals from Haxton and Lennie set up a thrilling finish for the Aberdeen support.

THURSDAY 27th SEPTEMBER 1956

Scotland international Steve Archibald was born in Glasgow. Archibald was signed by Aberdeen boss Billy McNeill in 1977 from Clyde in a £20,000 deal and went on to help his team to the league title in 1980, before moving to Tottenham Hotspur in an £800,000 transfer. After winning an FA Cup medal with Spurs, he was sold to Barcelona for £1.15m in August 1984. Archibald returned to Scotland and joined Hibernian and after his playing career he was involved with Airdrie and East Fife.

WEDNESDAY 27th SEPTEMBER 1972

Neutral Nuremberg was the venue for the Dons' Uefa Cup tie against Borussia Monchengladbach. The Bundesliga side became the first team to defeat Aberdeen at Pittodrie in a European tie in the first leg with a 3-2 win. At half-time in Germany, the Dons' incredibly levelled the tie on aggregate as Drew Jarvie, Willoughby and Steve Murray launched a blitz on the German defence. The Reds lost Henning Boel as he was stretchered off and they were eventually beaten by a late rally from Borussia in the final 20 minutes.

SATURDAY 28th SEPTEMBER 1968

Controversy as the bad feeling that prevailed between Aberdeen goalkeeper Bobby Clark and Celtic forward Bobby Lennox was once again in the headlines. Lennox had been involved in an unsavoury incident with Clark at Pittodrie a year previously and it was him again who was up to his tricks when he punched the ball out of Bobby Clark's hands before rolling it into the net. Furious protests by the whole Aberdeen side were in vain as Celtic won 2-1 before a stunned 35,000 Parkhead crowd.

WEDNESDAY 28TH SEPTEMBER 1977

Molenbeek ended Aberdeen hopes in the Uefa Cup with a 2-1 win at Pittodrie before a 26,000 attendance. Despite taking a 0-0 draw back from Belgium, the Dons were outclassed at times with Molenbeek's Boskamp showing his class. The result signalled the end for the likes of workmanlike Jim Shirra, as manager McNeill brought in the guile and promise of young Gordon Strachan from Dundee in the aftermath of the European exit.

SATURDAY 28TH SEPTEMBER 1985

Controversy as Rangers completely lost the plot against Aberdeen at Ibrox. The 37,600 crowd were howling with derision as two home players were sent off. Both Hugh Burns and Craig Paterson were sent off for appalling tackles and from one of the free-kicks awarded, Alex McLeish headed Aberdeen ahead. With only nine men, Rangers efforts were almost embarrassing as the Dons went on to win 3-0. In the second period the Dons played keep ball.

WEDNESDAY 29TH SEPTEMBER 1982

Taking a one-goal lead to Eastern Europe was never going to be an easy task for Aberdeen as they travelled to Albania for the return leg of the European Cup Winners' Cup tie. Tirana was sweltering in boiling temperatures as Aberdeen sat back and adopted a defensive strategy that Tirana could not break down. The 0-0 draw was job done for the Dons, who could now expect to face more formidable opponents in the latter rounds.

SATURDAY 30TH SEPTEMBER 1905

In a day that was to be remembered as 'Black Saturday' for Aberdeen. The first team were well beaten at Paisley as St Mirren won 4-2 while the Dons reserve side that had promised so much were hammered 9-0 against Hearts at Tynecastle in a 2nd XI Cup fixture. The local press was inundated with irate supporters voicing their concerns and aimed their anger at the Aberdeen directors.

TUESDAY 30th SEPTEMBER 1947

Former Aberdeen captain Jim Hermiston was born in Edinburgh. 'Hermit' as he became known, was one of Eddie Turnbull's first signings from Bonnyrigg Rose. After playing in the Dons side that won the Scottish Cup in 1970, Hermiston took over as Aberdeen captain when Steve Murray joined Celtic in 1973. Following his omission from the Scotland squad for the 1974 World Cup, despite being assured of a place, Hermiston became disillusioned with the game and he announced his retirement from football in 1975, taking up a position with Grampian Police.

WEDNESDAY 30th SEPTEMBER 1970

European history was made in Budapest as Aberdeen became the first side to be eliminated after a first-ever penalty shoot-out. Confusion reigned amongst the German officials as they were convinced that a third game was required between Aberdeen and Honved. A goal from Steve Murray hauled the Dons back into the game as they complained bitterly about two goals that were allowed by the referee with the linesman flagging for offside. It was Honved goalkeeper Bicskei who scored the decisive penalty to knock Aberdeen out of the competition. Earlier at two penalties each, Jim Forrest hit the bar with his effort.

WEDNESDAY 30th SEPTEMBER 1981

Ipswich boss Bobby Robson claimed after the Dons' first leg draw at Portman Road that Aberdeen could not play any better; he was wrong. In a memorable European night at Pittodrie, two second-half goals from Peter Weir put Aberdeen through to the next round of the Uefa Cup after a 3-1 win. In the build-up to the game, there had been comments made from Ipswich that had infuriated some of the Aberdeen players and staff. It was all the motivation needed as the Dons set about the holders with a passionate home support behind them.

ABERDEEN FC
On This Day

OCTOBER

SATURDAY 1st OCTOBER 1904

George Ritchie was dropped from the side following an unsavoury incident after Aberdeen had been held to a 1-1 draw against Aberdeen University in the Qualifying Cup. Ritchie had a reputation for being outspoken. The incident with an opposing player was never revealed in full detail but the club took a dim view of Ritchie's actions. After the Dons won the replay 6-1, he was restored to the side and scored both goals in vital 2-1 Qualifying Cup win at Cowdenbeath.

SATURDAY 1st OCTOBER 1955

Rangers were beaten 2-1 in the League Cup semi-final at Hampden Park. Aberdeen had dominated the first-half and went in at the break two goals ahead. The Dons relied on the pace of Leggat and Buckley up front and they proved to be the difference in the opening period. Rangers renowned 'Iron Curtain' defence had no answer to a slick Aberdeen forward line but the Glaswegians rallied in the second period after Leggat was rushed to hospital with an injured shoulder. Aberdeen showed they could defend in depth as they stood firm to claim their place in the final.

TUESDAY 1st OCTOBER 1963

Eric Black of Gothenburg fame was born in Bellshill. One of a host of youngsters that came through under the early days of Alex Ferguson, Black scored the Dons' opening goal in the 1983 European Cup Winners' Cup Final win over Real Madrid. Black was also on target 10 days later when he scored the winner against Rangers in the Scottish Cup Final. In 1986 he left Aberdeen to join Metz in France, much to the dismay of Alex Ferguson who dropped him for the final against Hearts. Black went on to make two appearances for Scotland before injury forced a premature retirement from playing. Black was assistant manager to Steve Bruce at Wigan in August 2008.

WEDNESDAY 1st OCTOBER 1980

A superb rearguard action by the Dons – described as their best defensive display on foreign soil – came in a 0-0 draw against Austria Memphis in Vienna. In the Dons' first European Champions Cup tie, Willie Miller was superb as he held the Austrians at bay before a 37,000 crowd at the same venue where the 2008 European Championships Final was held.

SATURDAY 2nd OCTOBER 1982

A crucial win for Aberdeen as they came back to snatch a last-gasp win against Motherwell at Pittodrie. The visitors had gone ahead through Edvaldsson on 25 minutes. It was not until substitute Steve Cowan hauled the Dons back into the game after the hour that Aberdeen looked like taking anything from the game. In the final minute a superb overhead kick from captain Willie Miller deceived Sproat to give the Dons a 2-1 win, and only their second league win in five games.

WEDNESDAY 3rd OCTOBER 1979

Brave Aberdeen went down 1-0 to Frankfurt in their Uefa Cup return tie in Germany. It took a goal from Holzenbein to knock Aberdeen out in the Wald Stadium in Frankfurt. Both Joe Harper and John McMaster went close for Aberdeen and Korean winger Cha Bum Cum almost scored a second in the final minute as the Dons threw everything at the Germans.

WEDNESDAY 3rd OCTOBER 1984

Disaster for Aberdeen as they went out of the European Cup against Dynamo Berlin, 5-4 on penalties. Ian Angus scored after 67 minutes to keep the Dons ahead, but when the Germans scored with just six minutes left, the game concluded with extra time and the inevitable penalty shoot-out. Willie Miller had the chance to put Aberdeen through had he scored; he didn't and then Black missed as the Dons went out at the first hurdle.

SATURDAY 4TH OCTOBER 1902

Orion welcomed Dundee 'A' to Cattofield in a Northern League fixture that ended in a riot. The visitors won 2-1 but their tactics and rough approach to the game won them few friends in the crowd. As the game ended, the Dundee players were subjected to abuse and stones being hurled from the crowd. Further down the road at Pittodrie, Aberdeen drew 1-1 with Arbroath in a Northern League fixture.

THURSDAY 4TH OCTOBER 2007

Ukraine was the destination for Aberdeen as they faced FC Dnipro in the opening round of the Uefa Cup. With a lucrative group stage place up for grabs, the smart money was on Dnipro finishing the job after the teams had finished 0-0 at Pittodrie. Darren Mackie scored for the Dons and from that point on the Reds had to defend in depth and hold on. Aberdeen progressed on the away goals rule after a 1-1 draw; the first time that Aberdeen had done so in Europe.

SATURDAY 5TH OCTOBER 1957

Graham Leggat was missing from the Aberdeen side as he was away with Scotland, scoring the Scots goal in a 1-1 draw against Northern Ireland in Belfast. Back at Pittodrie, transfer-seeking Hughie Hay scored three as Aberdeen defeated Airdrie 5-1 before a 10,000 crowd. Leggat was one of the few players left from the side that won the league title two years previously.

SATURDAY 6TH OCTOBER 1956

An incredible game as Aberdeen threw away a three-goal lead to East Fife in Methil. After 48 minutes the Dons looked out of sight as Bob Wishart put the visitors ahead 3-0. A win for the Dons would have hauled them up to second place; however, a spirited fight-back – and with the visitors' defence crumbling – the Fifers went on to claim both points before a 7,000 crowd.

SATURDAY 7TH OCTOBER 1882

Scottish Cup football arrived in Aberdeen when Dundee Harp visited in a first round tie. Around 400 hardy souls braved the elements to see the visitors win 3-1 in the original Aberdeen Football Club's first-ever Scottish Cup outing. The game was played at the Grammar School grounds in the centre of Aberdeen. This was the only enclosed venue available at that time.

SATURDAY 7TH OCTOBER 1939

More than 5,000 turned out to see the Aberdeen reserve side beat St Johnstone 8-2 in a second XI Cup match at Pittodrie. Matt Armstrong and Billy Strauss were in the side for what proved to be their last game for a while. Two days later they joined Andy Cowie as they joined the Royal Army Service Corp.

SATURDAY 8TH OCTOBER 1881

The Albert Hall in Aberdeen provided the setting for fourteen football enthusiasts as they set about forming the original Aberdeen Football Club. Three teachers from Woodside School instigated the initial procedures. A committee was formed and the new secretary instructed to buy a set of maroon jerseys, two balls and one inflator.

SATURDAY 8TH OCTOBER 1955

The league flag is unfurled at Pittodrie for the first time in the club's history before the Dons game against Queen of the South. The reason for the delay in the ceremony was due to the Aberdeen chairman being on holiday! The Dons continued their championship form with a 3-2 win that kept them at the top of the table.

SATURDAY 8TH OCTOBER 1966

Martin Buchan made his debut for Aberdeen against Dunfermline at East End Park in a 1-1 draw against the Fife side. Buchan was highly regarded by manager Eddie Turnbull and helped the Dons to a 1-1 draw by marking Dunfermline play-maker Alec Edwards throughout the game. Ally Shewan scored in the final minute after Harry Melrose had been sent off against his old club.

SATURDAY 8TH OCTOBER 1977

Alex Ferguson's St Mirren side had not lost at home since Aberdeen won a League Cup tie at Paisley more than a year ago. On this occasion, the Dons blew the Saints away in a 4-0 win that put them clear at the top of the table. Drew Jarvie helped himself to three goals as the Dons incisive attacks paid dividends in front of 12,900 fans.

SATURDAY 9TH OCTOBER 1982

Celtic lost their first league game of the season as Aberdeen showed their potential in a memorable 3-1 win. Celtic boss Billy McNeill was an animated character on the sidelines as Aberdeen took the lead through a Gordon Strachan penalty on 54 minutes. With the score at 2-1 for the Dons, home defender Danny McGrain was sent off after taking a swipe at his tormentor-in-chief, Peter Weir. Mark McGhee rattled in a third with four minutes to go to compound Celtic's misery.

WEDNESDAY 9TH OCTOBER 1985

The League Cup was the only trophy that had eluded Alex Ferguson during his time at Aberdeen and the Dons boss insisted that his side set that record straight. An Eric Black goal was enough to take a first leg semi-final lead back to Pittodrie against Dundee United. The Reds finished the job in style with Frank McDougall scoring the only goal of the game to put Aberdeen through to the final against Hibernian before a capacity 20,550 crowd.

SATURDAY 10TH OCTOBER 1903

The first-ever reserve game played by Aberdeen as Citadel 'A' were beaten 2-0. The Aberdeen second XI took their bow before a 2,000 crowd at Pittodrie. The home side were wearing different colours from the first XI and lined up thus: Willox, C Mackie, J Mackie, Murphy, Thomson, Catto, Clark, Rennie, Ruddiman, Wilson and Barron.

FRANK MCDOUGALL IN ACTION AGAINST PAUL HEGARTY IN THE 1985 LEAGUE CUP SEMI-FINAL AT PITTODRIE

SATURDAY 10TH OCTOBER 1908

Aberdeen went to the top of the league for the first time in their history following a 3-2 defeat of Partick Thistle at Pittodrie. Willie Lennie scored one of the goals as Aberdeen took over from Celtic at the top. The game was due to be played at Firhill but, as the ground was not fit for action, the game was switched to Pittodrie.

SATURDAY 10TH OCTOBER 1953

Hamilton was the latest side to fall to the Dons after a 5-1 win at Pittodrie. Paddy Buckley showed why the club paid £7,500 for him from St Johnstone with three goals in 15 second-half minutes. Aberdeen had made a poor start to the season but were making up for lost time against their fellow strugglers.

SATURDAY 11TH OCTOBER 1924

Aberdeen competed in the Highland League that season and it was the Don's reserve team that came up against Forres at Pittodrie and hammered the Highland side 9-0. Aberdeen went on to win the Highland League title that season, repeating the feat of 1912/13.

SATURDAY 11TH OCTOBER 1952

The Dons managed to win their first game of the season after a poor start to their league campaign. Third Lanark had proved to be a difficult side for the Dons with Aberdeen losing their previous five matches against the Cathkin Park side. They almost threw this one away: after being four goals up they were pegged back to hold out for a 4-3 win. The club announced that Jackie Allister was joining them from Chelsea in a £7,500 deal.

SATURDAY 12TH OCTOBER 1957

Fresh from scoring for Scotland, Aberdeen winger Graham Leggat showed his true class, hitting five of the Dons goals in the 6-2 win over Airdrie at Broomfield. Leggat ran amok after putting the Dons ahead in the 19th minute. The convincing win sent Airdrie to the foot of the table.

WEDNESDAY 12TH OCTOBER 1974

A first venture into the Texaco Cup for Aberdeen ended with a defeat against Newcastle United at St James' Park. After a 1-1 draw at Pittodrie, the Dons went down 3-2 in the second leg. Billy Pirie scored for the Dons but it was his opposite number Malcolm MacDonald that caught the eye.

SATURDAY 13TH OCTOBER 1962

Raith Rovers were on the end of a real hammering from Aberdeen as the Dons went on to record their biggest win since the war in a 10-0 victory. Raith were not surprisingly rooted at the bottom of the league, and it was Bobby Cummings who scored four of the Dons goals in the rout before a 9,000 attendance.

WEDNESDAY 13TH OCTOBER 1982

Jim Leighton made his Scotland debut against East Germany at Hampden. The Aberdeen goalkeeper went on to become the most capped custodian in Scotland with 91 international appearances that also included a record four World Cup Finals. Scotland won 2-0 to open their European Championship campaign.

SATURDAY 14TH OCTOBER 1905

Benny Yorston was born in Nigg. Yorston was signed from Mugiemoss before he first came to the attention of manager Travers during the club tour to South Africa in 1927. He went on to become the club record scorer with 38 goals in season 1929/30. After receiving a full cap for Scotland in 1931, he was one of five Aberdeen players caught up in a betting scandal – the 'Great Mystery' – and was sold to Sunderland some months later.

WEDNESDAY 14TH OCTOBER 1942

Charlie Cooke, the Dons winger from the early 1960s, was born in St Monace in Fife. Cooke was the jewel in the Aberdeen crown in a struggling side. It was with great disappointment that Cooke was allowed to join Dundee for £44,000 in 1964. Cooke went on to play for Chelsea. Latterly, he was part of the Coerver Coaching set up in the USA.

SATURDAY 14th OCTOBER 1972

Its was debut time for new signing Zoltan Varga, who made an immediate impact at Pittodrie with his array of skills. Varga showed that he was real class in the 2-2 draw with Falkirk. Never one that would win any loyalty bonuses, Varga was banned from playing in Germany which prompted his move to Aberdeen. Varga's stay in Scotland was all too brief and he was sold to Ajax for £40,000 in 1973 as a replacement for none other than Johan Cruyff.

SATURDAY 15th OCTOBER 1963

Falkirk were beaten in the Dons' first home win of the season in a 3-0 victory. It was a much-changed Aberdeen side as Bobby Cummings was sold to Newcastle for £5,000, with Willie Allan going to St Mirren in exchange for Don Kerrigan. With only John Ogston and captain Kinnell the only ever-presents, the changes had an effect as the Dons cruised to victory before a poor 8,000 crowd.

TUESDAY 15th OCTOBER 1996

Zalgiris Vilnius and Welsh side Barry Town were both beaten as Aberdeen made progress in the Uefa Cup. Next up for the Dons was Ebbe Skovdahl's Brondby side. The Danes had previous Champions League experience and that showed as they eased to a 2-0 win at Pittodrie before a poor 14,159 attendance. Aberdeen managed a 0-0 draw in the return but never threatened to get back into the tie at any stage.

SATURDAY 16th OCTOBER 1999

Ebbe Skovdahl was left with his new side in tatters after being humiliated 7-0 against Celtic at Parkhead. It was the Dons worst ever result in the Premier League and one that confirmed Aberdeen as the bottom side in the league. This was the Dons' sixth game of the season, and with only one point to show for their efforts, Skovdahl presided over the worst ever start to a season.

SATURDAY 17TH OCTOBER 1959

After just 15 seconds of the Dons game against Kilmarnock at Rugby Park, Dons captain Archie Glen clashed with Willie Toner. Both were carried off and it was the end of a memorable career for Glen. As part of the famed Allister, Young and Glen half-back line of the 1950s, Archie was also capped for Scotland after making his first Aberdeen appearance against Falkirk in February 1950.

SATURDAY 17TH OCTOBER 1970

Aberdonian Colin Jackson, the Rangers defender, sliced the ball past his own keeper to give the Dons the lead at Ibrox. Despite the good fortune, it was no more than the Reds deserved as they went on to a comfortable 2-0 win when Joe Harper's goal on 58 minutes triggered a mass exodus from the Ibrox stands.

SATURDAY 18TH OCTOBER 1952

A sensational game at Broomfield as Aberdeen eventually racked up their highest league tally since the war in a 7-4 win over Airdrie. After 20 minutes, the game was tied at 4-4. Three Aberdeen players – Hamilton, Buckley and Hather – all scored two goals each as the Dons took control in the second period.

WEDNESDAY 19TH OCTOBER 1966

For the second season in succession, Aberdeen lost out to Rangers in a semi-final at Hampden Park. This time it was the League Cup as the Dons battled to a 2-2 draw before a 38,600 attendance. Jimmy Smith was booked for the third time that season as tempers frayed. The new substitute rule was brought into question as both clubs used a replacement in extra time.

WEDNESDAY 19TH OCTOBER 1983

Belgian side Beveren were the form team as they welcomed Aberdeen for this European Cup Winners' Cup tie. Top of the Belgian league and undefeated in ten games, they came up against a side that had enough experience in the European arena to handle anything that the Belgians could come up with. A 0-0 draw was satisfactory for Aberdeen.

WEDNESDAY 20th OCTOBER 1982

Polish league leaders Lech Poznan arrived in Aberdeen looking to set up their own defensive shell against a free-scoring Aberdeen in their second round European Cup Winners' Cup tie at Pittodrie. The 17,600 crowd were frustrated at the opponent's tactics of stopping play at every opportunity. When the Dons did get the chance to play, they only had two goals to show for their efforts, which was a satisfactory result given the quality of the opposition.

WEDNESDAY 20th OCTOBER 1993

After comfortably getting past Icelandic side Valur in the opening round, Aberdeen came up against Italian side Torino at Pittodrie in the second round of the European Cup Winners' Cup. The Dons shocked the Italians as they raced into a 2-0 lead. Eventually, the Dons were pinned back but still had high hopes of progressing after a narrow 3-2 defeat.

WEDNESDAY 20th OCTOBER 1999

A remarkable game and a first league win of the season for Aberdeen after ten games. Motherwell welcomed the Dons to Fir Park looking to pile on the misery for a side that had just lost by seven goals to Celtic. Aberdeen would eventually prevail in an incredible game that ended in a 6-5 win for the Dons.

WEDNESDAY 21st OCTOBER 1908

The Robertson Cup was inaugurated once again. Previously the cup had been competed for in the late 1890s and the competition was resurrected with Aberdeen, Dundee, Falkirk and Airdrie competing. It was decided that it would be the Dons reserve side that would represent the club.

SATURDAY 21st OCTOBER 1961

Aberdeen ended one of their worst sequences of results since the war with a 1-0 win at Falkirk. The Dons had lost their previous four matches, conceding 15 goals. John Ogston replaced Chris Harker in goal in an attempt to arrest the decline and Billy Little's goal on 67 minutes gave Aberdeen the vital win to ease their relegation fears.

DUNCAN SHEARER IN ACTION AGAINST TORINO AT PITTODRIE IN THE 1993 ECWC TIE.

WEDNESDAY 21st OCTOBER 1981

The Dons took a giant step towards qualifying past the second round of a European tournament for the first time after a comprehensive 3-0 win over Romanian side Arges Pitesti. Three goals ahead by the interval, Aberdeen should have been out of sight but for a succession of missed chances later in the game. The 22,000 crowd were happy enough that the Dons would take their lead to what was certainly going to be a tough return in Romania.

SATURDAY 22nd OCTOBER 1910

Only 7,500 turned out to see Aberdeen maintain their unbeaten start to the 1910/11 season. A goal from winger Jimmy Soye gave the Dons a 1-0 win over Airdrie at Pittodrie in the club's tenth game in a row undefeated. Aberdeen had only dropped points in drawn matches against Third Lanark, Hamilton and Clyde.

SATURDAY 22nd OCTOBER 1955

As the only undefeated side in Britain, Aberdeen went into the League Cup Final against St Mirren with confidence that came from being the league champions, and from enjoying a long unbeaten run. It was Graham Leggat that conjured up a magical winning goal to take the cup to Pittodrie. More than 15,000 supporters crammed into the Aberdeen Joint station late in the evening as the players returned from Hampden Park.

WEDNESDAY 22nd OCTOBER 1980

Described as the biggest game in Pittodrie history, the Dons went down 1-0 against Liverpool in their European Cup second round tie. Billed as a "Battle of Britain", the influential John McMaster was off the field receiving treatment which allowed McDermott to score for Liverpool. Once he returned, he was taken out by Kennedy and was lost to the Dons for more than a year. It was reported that the club could have sold more than 60,000 tickets for the game, such was the interest.

SUNDAY 22ND OCTOBER 1989

Paul Mason scored twice as Aberdeen defeated Rangers to lift the League Cup. The sides had clashed in each of the previous two finals and although they had been described as classics, Rangers won both. The Dons under Willie Miller were determined to finish the 1980s on a high, and after extra time it was Aberdeen that deservedly won. It was Miller's last success as Aberdeen captain.

WEDNESDAY 23RD OCTOBER 1968

Real Zaragoza were the Dons opponents in this Inter Cities Fairs Cup meeting at Pittodrie. An unfortunate own goal from Tom McMillan on 73 minutes was a lucky break for the visitors who were under pressure from Aberdeen for most of the game. The Dons had missed talismanic Dave Robb who was not risked due to an injury before the game as Aberdeen took a 2-1 lead to Spain.

SATURDAY 23RD OCTOBER 1976

Aberdeen went clear at the top of the league after a memorable 2-1 win over Celtic at Pittodrie. The 19,400 crowd were treated to a classic as Celtic opened the scoring through a Dalglish penalty on 56 minutes. From that point on Aberdeen laid siege to the visitors' goal and they were eventually rewarded when Harper converted a penalty after Latchford had brought down Arthur Graham.

SUNDAY 23RD OCTOBER 1988

A classic League Cup Final as Aberdeen lost 3-2 to Rangers as the sides clashed in the final for the second year in a row. Two goals from Davie Dodds were not enough as the Dons went down before a 72,122 crowd.

SATURDAY 24TH OCTOBER 1970

Aberdeen cruised to a comfortable 3-1 win over St Mirren at Love Street to keep the Dons in contention at the top of the table with Celtic. When Hamilton rounded Bobby Clark to score a consolation for the home side in 79 minutes, it was to be the last goal that Aberdeen would concede until the 16th January.

WEDNESDAY 24TH OCTOBER 1973

Tottenham visited Pittodrie for the Dons' first-ever competitive tie against English opposition in the second round of the Uefa Cup. Spurs were previous winners of both the Uefa and Cup Winners' Cup in the past and they withstood an Aberdeen onslaught to survive with a tense 1-1 draw before a 30,000 Pittodrie crowd. A late Jim Hermiston penalty gave the Dons hope but they went down 4-1 at White Hart Lane in the return.

TUESDAY 24TH OCTOBER 1995

Eoin Jess was in majestic form as he helped Aberdeen to a 2-1 win over Rangers that took Aberdeen through to the League Cup Final. Jess and Paul Bernard were up against Paul Gascoigne but it was two goals from Billy Dodds that helped Aberdeen to victory. Jess took the time out in the closing minutes to play some 'keepy-up' with the ball to the delight of the Aberdeen support in the 26,131 crowd.

SATURDAY 25TH OCTOBER 1952

East Fife arrived at Pittodrie as league leaders having dropped only one point all season. Unpredictable Aberdeen set about destroying the Fife hopes with a sensational 6-3 victory. After Hamilton scored from a penalty to put Aberdeen 4-2 ahead, East Fife's Duncan missed a penalty to boost Aberdeen hopes. Former Dons Don Emery and John Curran were in the visitors' side before a 20,000 attendance.

SATURDAY 26TH OCTOBER 1957

Disaster for Aberdeen as they not only lost at home to Partick Thistle but star forward and Scotland international Graham Leggat broke his leg, ruling him out until February. Leggat had been in inspired form and was also the only Aberdeen player established in the Scotland side before a poor tackle with Baird left the Dons player writhing in agony. The Reds 3-1 defeat followed on from a heavy defeat against Hearts.

SATURDAY 27TH OCTOBER 1906

Aberdeen fielded three teams on the same day for the first time. As the first team were recording their first away win of the season in a 3-1 win at Kilmarnock, Arbroath were beaten 2-0 at Pittodrie in Northern league fixture by Aberdeen 'A'. Over at Central Park in Kittybrewster the third team were held in a 2-2 draw against East End in a county cup-tie.

WEDNESDAY 27TH OCTOBER 1971

A partisan 35,000 crowd at the Communale Stadium in Turin helped Juventus to take a 2-0 lead in the Uefa Cup second round tie, first leg. Aberdeen were up against the most expensive team in world football and at times struggled with the Italians' slick passing and movement. Dons defender Willie Young was taken off in the second half to save him from being sent off. Several Aberdeen players were surprised that they were not allowed to tackle the Italians as the Bulgarian referee was protecting the home players too much.

WEDNESDAY 27TH OCTOBER 1976

Rangers were beaten 5-1 by Aberdeen as the Dons reached the League Cup Final in style. Only 20,990 were at Hampden for the Dons goal-fest as Aberdeen, under manager Ally MacLeod, swept aside the Rangers challenge. Jocky Scott was the third Dons player to score a hat-trick against the Blues, after Joe O'Neil and Bobby Cummings managed the feat in the 1950s and 1960s.

SUNDAY 27TH OCTOBER 1985

The one trophy that had eluded Alex Ferguson during his spell with Aberdeen was secured after a one-sided League Cup Final against Hibernian at Hampden Park. In what became known as the '13-minute' final; that was all the time it took for Aberdeen to finish the game as a contest with early goals from Eric Black and Billy Stark. John Hewitt was the sponsors' man-of-the-match before a 40,050 crowd.

SATURDAY 28TH OCTOBER 1972

Bobby Clark had submitted a transfer request as Stoke City closed in on a replacement for Gordon Banks. Aberdeen then lost to Celtic for the first time in years as two sublime goals from Zoltan Varga were not enough to prevent the Dons going down 3-2 before a 33,000 Pittodrie crowd. Hungarian international Varga's second goal was a superb lob from 25 yards – hailed as the finest ever seen at Pittodrie.

SATURDAY 29TH OCTOBER 1983

Aberdeen went top of the league after a 3-1 win over Dundee at Dens Park. Goals from Strachan, Weir and Bell eased the Dons past a Dundee side that included a young Stewart McKimmie. The Aberdeen support in the 7,800 crowd were more concerned at news of Rangers' latest attempt to lure Alex Ferguson to take over at Ibrox. The Aberdeen boss remained tight-lipped on the speculation, but the Dons' support made their feelings known by chanting his name throughout the game. The board then began negotiations to keep hold of their manager by offering him a new deal.

WEDNESDAY 30TH OCTOBER 1968

Real Zaragoza gave Aberdeen a lesson in European football as they cruised to a 3-0 win in the intimidating Romareda Stadium as the Dons were knocked out of the Fairs Cup. Zaragoza were previous winners and they continued their run of never having lost to a British side on Spanish soil. Aberdeen had taken a 2-1 lead to Spain; Zaragoza would fall to eventual winners Newcastle United in the next round.

SATURDAY 31ST OCTOBER 1885

Orion played their first-ever match when they held the original Aberdeen to a 2-2 draw at the Recreation Grounds in the city. Orion took their name from Latin and Greek language and was known as a giant in Greek mythology. Led by William Jaffrey they went on to form the present Aberdeen FC along with Aberdeen and Victoria United.

ABERDEEN FC
On This Day

NOVEMBER

SATURDAY 1st NOVEMBER 1902

A move by Hibernian in Edinburgh to relocate their side to Aberdeen and effectively take over the club was fiercely resisted by the Dons board of directors. Hibs had gone into great detail over the move and even sent a valuer north to carry out a survey. This was met with strong opposition by Aberdeen and it was on the back of this bid that the amalgamation process was hastened.

WEDNESDAY 1st NOVEMBER 1978

Fortuna Dusseldorf lived up to their name by holding out in fortuitous circumstances against an Aberdeen onslaught that deserved more. After losing the first game in Germany 3-0 in their European Cup Winners' Cup tie, manager Ferguson removed any defensive thoughts from his side in an all-out effort to rescue the tie. Two goals in three second-half minutes set up an exciting finale where the Germans held on as the 16,800 crowd urged the Dons on in a frantic closing spell.

SATURDAY 1st NOVEMBER 1975

Aberdeen defeated Dundee in what would prove to be a crucial win in the first season of the new 10-team Premier league. The Dons had been struggling but goals from former Dundee player Jocky Scott, and a Billy Williamson penalty in two second-half minutes, gave the Dons a deserved 2-0 win over fellow relegation strugglers Dundee.

TUESDAY 2nd NOVEMBER 1976

Four days before Aberdeen were due to meet Celtic in the League Cup Final, the Dons played Motherwell at Pittodrie in the league. Dons boss Ally MacLeod could not rest any of his stars before the game as his side were sitting at the top of the league. Late goals from Drew Jarvie, Sullivan and Harper sent the 15,200 fans home happy. Next stop Hampden.

WEDNESDAY 2ND NOVEMBER 1983

Alex Ferguson pulled off a masterstroke by announcing before the start that he was not joining Rangers and signing a new contract with Aberdeen, as the Dons prepared to face Beveren in their European Cup Winners' Cup tie. The game turned into a celebration as Aberdeen cruised past the Belgian league leaders in a 4-1 win before a 21,000 attendance.

MONDAY 3RD NOVEMBER 1975

Ally MacLeod was appointed new Aberdeen manager after the departure of Jim Bonthrone. MacLeod was a winger with Blackburn Rovers in his playing days and had been successful in taking Ayr United into the new Premier League set up in Scotland. MacLeod arrived in a blaze of publicity and openly declared that Aberdeen would win a major trophy within a year. He was true to his word as the Dons won the League Cup almost exactly 12 months later 'Super Ally' – as he became known by the Aberdeen support – was only at Pittodrie for an 18-month spell before being appointed Scotland coach in May 1977.

WEDNESDAY 3RD NOVEMBER 1982

A passionate crowd of 30,000 believed that their Poznan side could claw back the two goals conceded against Aberdeen at Pittodrie in their European Cup Winners' Cup tie. With Aberdeen in no mood to give anything away, they never looked in danger against a side that would go on to win the Polish league that year. When Doug Bell rolled the ball over the line on 59 minutes, the tie was effectively over. Aberdeen had qualified for the quarter-finals in Europe for the first time.

MONDAY 3RD NOVEMBER 1986

The last game that Alex Ferguson took charge at Aberdeen was in the relatively low-key setting of Inverness. The Dons defeated Caley 5-1 in a centenary match for the Inverness club. Three days later Ferguson was to be appointed as the new manager of Manchester United.

WEDNESDAY 3rd NOVEMBER 1993

Aberdeen took the lead for the third time against Torino in their European Cup Winners' Cup tie when Lee Richardson scored a spectacular goal before a capacity 21,655 Pittodrie crowd. Torino hit back and eventually knocked Aberdeen out 5-3 on aggregate in what was the Dons final tie in the tournament.

WEDNESDAY 4th NOVEMBER 1959

Floodlights were switched on for only the second time at Pittodrie with the visit of Arsenal as the Dons got used to playing evening matches. The Gunners arrived in Aberdeen with their hosts still smarting from a 7-2 defeat at Clyde; their worst result for 30 years. A crowd of 11,000 were present as the Londoners ran out comfortable 2-1 winners with Jim Clunie scoring a late penalty for Aberdeen.

WEDNESDAY 4th NOVEMBER 1981

Despite taking a 3-0 lead to Romania for their second round Uefa Cup tie, the Dons found themselves in trouble at the break against Arges Pitesti as they went in 2-0 down. It was in the Pitesti ground that Alex Ferguson infamously kicked a tea urn that was full to the brim during his half-time 'talk' to his players. Grimacing with pain Fergie carried on and his players responded in style to level the tie at 2-2 and go through to the third round of a European competition for the first time.

WEDNESDAY 4th NOVEMBER 1987

After defeating Irish side Bohemians in the first round, the Dons came up against Dutch side Feyenoord in the Uefa Cup. After a 2-1 win at Pittodrie, Aberdeen were bitterly disappointed to go down by a single goal in Rotterdam and out on away goals.

WEDNESDAY 5th NOVEMBER 1884

Peterhead Football Club were formed, a board of directors were appointed, and their colours chosen as blue. Several months later they played their first-ever game when they welcomed Aberdeen to the Links, losing on 21st March 1885.

SATURDAY 5TH NOVEMBER 1904

Augustus Lowe was a player that would never appear in a list of Aberdeen legends, but he certainly made an impact on his debut. Lowe scored all four goals in his first appearance in a 4-1 win over East Stirlingshire at Pittodrie in a Northern League match. Lowe went on to play only three games for the club, scoring six goals in the process.

TUESDAY 5TH NOVEMBER 1963

Dutch international and Dons' record signing, Hans Gillhaus, was born in Helmond in Holland. Gillhaus joined Aberdeen from PSV Eindhoven in a £650,000 transfer in November 1989. A European Cup winner with PSV, Gillhaus was an immediate success at Pittodrie as he formed a lethal partnership with Charlie Nicholas that brought both the domestic cups to Pittodrie in the 1989/90 season.

WEDNESDAY 5TH NOVEMBER 1980

Scottish champions Aberdeen were handed a European lesson from Liverpool as the Dons were crushed 4-0 in a European Cup tie at Anfield. It was always going to be a tough task for the Dons who trailed 1-0 from the first game at Pittodrie. After Mark McGhee missed an early opportunity, there was no way back as Liverpool took command with two goals before the break. Drew Jarvie, the experienced Aberdeen forward, was quoted as saying to his teammates at half time; "Come on lads, just three quick goals and we are back in it!"

SATURDAY 6TH NOVEMBER 1976

The League Cup was won for the second time after a 2-1 win over Celtic at Hampden Park. It was a first success for Aberdeen captain Willie Miller. Goals from Drew Jarvie and substitute Davie Robb took the cup to Pittodrie. Manager Ally MacLeod had promised a trophy in his first year in charge and he duly delivered. Aberdeen goalkeeper Bobby Clark revealed that he had dreamt the night before the game that Robb would come on and score the winner.

SATURDAY 8TH NOVEMBER 1980

Aberdeen dug in at the top of the league after an impressive 2-0 win at Celtic, their nearest challengers. Mark McGhee set up strikes in each half for Walker McCall. The 29,000 crowd grew impatient as they watched their side being outclassed. Tempers boiled over and Gordon Strachan was subjected to an attack from a Celtic supporter, who charged at him across the field in the second half.

THURSDAY 8TH NOVEMBER 2007

Russian giants Lokomotiv Moscow came up against stubborn resistance from Aberdeen in their Uefa Cup Group B match at Pittodrie. Zander Diamond put the Dons ahead before Moscow levelled just before the break. Lokomotiv had been spending big in recent months to improve their squad but were content to hold on for a draw against an Aberdeen side that still had hopes of qualifying from their group.

SATURDAY 9TH NOVEMBER 1957

The unusual sight of an RAF band on the field before the start was welcome pre-match entertainment for the 10,000 crowd. Thereafter, it was the Aberdeen forwards that entertained with five goals in an impressive 5-2 win over Queen's Park at Pittodrie. Norman Davidson showed all of his power and pace to score three goals. Two late strikes from the visitors did not detract from the Dons domination.

WEDNESDAY 10TH NOVEMBER 1971

Exactly 34 years to the day when Scotland last played at Pittodrie, the Scots broke with tradition and played Belgium in Aberdeen in a European Championship match. Hampden Park had been the Scots preferred venue since before the war. The SFA took the view that Pittodrie would be a more intimidating place for the Belgians and a solitary John O'Hare goal was enough to give Scotland a 1-0 win. Kenny Dalglish made his international debut that night. Bobby Clark, Martin Buchan and Steve Murray from Aberdeen were all in the side with Jim Forrest listed as one of the substitutes.

SATURDAY 11TH NOVEMBER 1995

After knocking Rangers out of the League Cup at the semi-final stage, the Dons travelled to Ibrox and continued to frustrate Rangers in a 1-1 draw. The Blues' Paul Gascoigne was lucky to stay on the field after a succession of nasty incidents. Eoin Jess scored one of his trademark goals to earn Aberdeen a point before a frenzied 45,427 Ibrox crowd.

SATURDAY 12TH NOVEMBER 1904

Aberdeen had won at Cowdenbeath in the Qualifying Cup and a home tie against Clyde in the semi-final captured the imagination of the Dons support. A record 12,000 turned out to see Aberdeen make it through to the final with a 1-0 win. The crowd paid £284, which was not exceeded by the international in 1900 due to the increased admission costs. There was plenty of bad feeling towards the Clyde players as they adopted crude tactics to stop Aberdeen and a post-match protest was lodged by the visitors. The SFA threw out the protest some days later.

SUNDAY 12TH NOVEMBER 1911

Matt Armstrong of 1930s fame was born in Newton Stewart. Armstrong went on to become one of the most accomplished players ever to play for the club and scored the Aberdeen goal in the 1937 Scottish Cup Final. Armstrong made his debut on the back of the 1931 scandal that saw five Aberdeen players dropped from the side and he kept his place until the outbreak of the war, which effectively ended his Dons career.

SATURDAY 12TH NOVEMBER 1983

Rangers arrived at Pittodrie in buoyant mood after Jock Wallace, their former manager, had returned for a second spell at Ibrox. Wallace insisted on his players reverting to their traditional red and black socks but it was Aberdeen that dominated proceedings. The Dons were the dominant force in Scotland and the 3-0 win could have been a lot worse for the visitors had it not been for some inspired goalkeeping.

THURSDAY 6TH NOVEMBER 1986

The end of an era at Pittodrie as Alex Ferguson departed to take over as manager at Manchester United. It brought an end to a seven-year spell that had been the most successful in Aberdeen FC's history. Ferguson arrived from St Mirren in 1978 and won four Scottish Cups, three league titles, one League Cup and the European Cup Winners' Cup and Super Cup.

SATURDAY 7TH NOVEMBER 1964

Rangers welcomed Aberdeen to Ibrox in the middle of a poor run that saw the Ibrox side slip into mid-table. Inconsistency meant that the Dons were looking towards the teams at the bottom. Despite losing Bennett through injury, Aberdeen took the lead at a fog-shrouded Ibrox and were good value for their 2-2 draw. It was a welcome boost for the Dons who had been beaten heavily at the same venue in the League Cup.

WEDNESDAY 7TH NOVEMBER 1973

Tottenham Hotspur proved too strong for Aberdeen in their return Uefa Cup clash at White Hart Lane. The Dons were held 1-1 in the first game at Pittodrie and two late goals from McGrath in London was harsh on the Reds who had more than held their own after Drew Jarvie scored in the 54th minute. It could have been different for Aberdeen as they were denied a clear penalty when referee Tshenscher gave the award, only to change his mind after protests from the Spurs players.

SATURDAY 8TH NOVEMBER 1952

The Aberdeen players that took the field against Raith Rovers at Kirkcaldy wore black armbands as a mark of respect following the death of popular goalkeeper Frank Watson. The young Don had been struck down for some time and passed away after contracting polio. Watson made his debut for Aberdeen against Celtic in a 5-1 win in January 1947.

SATURDAY 13th NOVEMBER 1971

As league leaders Aberdeen welcomed bottom-placed East Fife to Pittodrie there was sure to be only one outcome; the Dons pummelled the Fifers for the duration and the home side were good value for their 5-0 win. Ian Taylor and Jim Hermiston scored late goals to leave the Dons unbeaten at Pittodrie for two years.

SATURDAY 14th NOVEMBER 1953

Queen of the South arrived at Pittodrie as unlikely league leaders after only 11 games. Aberdeen had been bottom of the league after five matches and incredibly, after the Dons' 2-0 win, they went second behind the Dumfries side. The visitors had scored 31 goals in ten matches but after Jackie Hather volleyed past Henderson just before the interval it was Aberdeen that took control.

SATURDAY 15th NOVEMBER 1930

Alex Merrie created history when he scored six of Aberdeen's seven goals against Hibernian at Pittodrie. Merrie had been drafted in to replace the injured Benny Yorston and was soon back in the reserves despite his amazing scoring feat.

SATURDAY 16th NOVEMBER 1946

There was an air of despondency around Pittodrie as the team wore black arm bands for the visit of Queen's Park. Earlier in the week news came through that former player Alex Jackson was killed in a car crash in Cairo. Aberdeen kept in touch at the top of the table with a 3-1 win over the famous amateurs.

WEDNESDAY 17th NOVEMBER 1971

Italian side Juventus knocked Aberdeen out of the Uefa Cup after a 1-1 draw at Pittodrie was not enough for the Dons following a 2-0 first leg defeat in Turin. There had been plenty of acrimony between the clubs before the tie as dates for the matches could not be agreed upon. Aberdeen gave a good account of themselves at a snowbound Pittodrie and a 77th minute header from Joe Harper preserved the Dons unbeaten home record in Europe.

SATURDAY 17TH NOVEMBER 1984

Aberdeen inflicted more misery on Rangers as the Dons became the first side to win at Ibrox that season. Despite Rangers taking the lead through Mitchell, it was Aberdeen that responded by drawing level through Billy Stark after 19 minutes. Frank McDougall then grabbed his tenth goal of the season to give the Dons victory in front of a 44,000 attendance.

WEDNESDAY 18TH NOVEMBER 1931

A black day for Aberdeen as a terse statement issued by the club stated that five first team players, namely, Jimmy Black, Hugh McLaren, Frank Hill, Benny Yorston and David Galloway were dropped from the side and that none of them would ever play for the first team again. It emerged some time later that the players had been involved in a betting scam that was known locally as "the Great Mystery" mainly due to the reluctance of the club to reveal any details of the operation that was discovered. It was not until some 70 years later that details emerged but, to this day, the truth has never come out.

WEDNESDAY 19TH NOVEMBER 1986

Ian Porterfield was the surprise choice to take over as Aberdeen manager after Alex Ferguson joined Manchester United. Porterfield was legendary on Wearside for his winning goal in the 1973 FA Cup Final as Sunderland beat Leeds United against all the odds. Having spent almost his entire playing and coaching career in England, Porterfield's appointment was a surprise one by the Aberdeen board. He also appointed Jimmy Mullen as his assistant. Following after Alex Ferguson was perhaps the most difficult job in football. Porterfield's record at Aberdeen was as good as most of those that followed, but Aberdeen had lost the flair that had become their trademark under Ferguson.

SATURDAY 20TH NOVEMBER 1971

Despite going out of Europe against Juventus, Aberdeen bounced back with a 4-0 win over Motherwell at Fir Park. Steve Murray scored a goal in each half as the Dons kept in touch at the top of the table.

SATURDAY 21st NOVEMBER 1931

Youngster Matt Armstrong earned a quick promotion to the first team in the aftermath of the 'Great Mystery' betting scandal. Armstrong played in the black and golds' 3-0 defeat at Brockville in a side that showed several changes with five of the Aberdeen side – who were implicated in the scandal – never playing for the club again.

FRIDAY 21st NOVEMBER 1941

Long-serving player and trainer Donald Colman was put on sick leave by Aberdeen as ill-health had curtailed his involvement with the club he had served since 1907. The club announced that East End trainer Bobby Carroll would take over the role of trainer and groundsman at Pittodrie.

SATURDAY 21st NOVEMBER 1970

Struggling Hearts made Aberdeen battle all the way as a Joe Harper penalty gave the Dons their seventh successive win. With Celtic dropping a point at Falkirk, the Dons were now a point behind the Hoops at the top of the table. It was Harper who was pulled down in the box for the penalty. Despite being injured he took the spot-kick and lashed the ball high past Hearts goalkeeper Jim Cruickshank.

FRIDAY 21st NOVEMBER 1997

Alex Miller's ill-fated spell in charge began when he was unveiled as the new Aberdeen manager at Pittodrie. Several supporters groups had questioned the appointment as Miller had gained a reputation of being defensive in his approach in his previous time with Hibernian. Those fears were realised some 12 months later as Miller was sacked after a series of poor results and questionable signings. Among those was that of Craig Hignett who was reported to be the highest earner at the club, picking up in excess of £8,000 per week. Miller later joined Liverpool as a scout and latterly assisted Rafael Benitez at Anfield.

SATURDAY 22ND NOVEMBER 1952

Falkirk were the latest side to suffer at the hands of a free-scoring Aberdeen. The Dons 7-2 win over the Bairns saw their 33rd goal in seven matches. Reggie Morrison made his debut for Aberdeen as he took over from an injured Fred Martin in goal. All of the action was at the other end as the Dons scored six goals in a frantic second period.

SATURDAY 22ND NOVEMBER 1975

Ally MacLeod took charge for the first time at Pittodrie following his move from Ayr United. MacLeod had watched Aberdeen from the Fir Park stands two weeks earlier and was on the bench for the Dons 2-1 win at Tannadice. MacLeod announced that Aberdeen would play with a style and flair that was the Pittodrie tradition; his claims had to be put on hold as the Dons were held by Hearts to a 0-0 draw before a 11,400 crowd.

SATURDAY 22ND NOVEMBER 1980

Aberdeen completed a remarkable 30-game unbeaten run in the Premier League after a 1-1 draw against Kilmarnock at Rugby Park. The Dons had dominated the league since winning the championship in May 1980. It looked as though their unbeaten record was going as Kilmarnock held out until the final minute when Alex McLeish scored with a fierce header to save the Dons from an unlikely defeat.

TUESDAY 22ND NOVEMBER 1983

As European Cup holders, former adversaries Hamburg would meet European Cup Winners' Cup holders Aberdeen to contest the 1983 European Super Cup. Back then, the trophy was played for over two legs. The Dons showed the Germans they had learned quite a bit from their last clash in 1982 and should have taken more than the 0-0 scoreline back to Pittodrie for the second leg. Not for the first time, Aberdeen had travelled to Germany and enhanced their growing reputation in Europe.

SATURDAY 23RD NOVEMBER 1901

Aberdeen defeated local rivals Orion 2-1 at Pittodrie to advance in the Aberdeenshire Cup. It was the third occasion that the sides had clashed that season and tempers flared on the field in a heated local derby cup-tie. Meanwhile, down the coast old rivals Arbroath were playing a reserve game for the first time when they beat Aberdeen University 6-2 at Gayfield.

SATURDAY 24TH NOVEMBER 1979

The Dons completed a League Cup double over the Old Firm with a 1-0 win against Celtic at Parkhead. Taking a 3-2 lead from the first game at Pittodrie, Aberdeen finished the job when Mark McGhee scored the only goal of the game on 50 minutes. The only blemish on the Dons' copybook was a bad knee injury to Joe Harper which was eventually to end his memorable career with the club.

WEDNESDAY 25TH NOVEMBER 1959

Jim Bett, the Dons £300,000 signing from Lokeren in 1985, was born in Hamilton. Bett joined Aberdeen after the Dons had retained the Premier League and went on to win both domestic cups with the club in his first season. Capped for Scotland on 25 occasions, Bett left Aberdeen in 1994 after making 338 appearances for the club. Bett was also in the Scotland squads for the 1986 and 1990 World Cup Finals.

WEDNESDAY 25TH NOVEMBER 1970

Polish side Gornik Zabrze arrived for their short tour of Scotland with a big reputation. With games lined up against Aberdeen, Hearts and Falkirk, the Poles were taken apart by a slick Dons side that won 5-0 before a 17,618 crowd. Aberdeen had been seen as a team that was well suited for European football and they showed what they were capable of with five different scorers against a side that were seasoned European campaigners.

WEDNESDAY 25TH NOVEMBER 1981

Franz Beckenbauer was with Hamburg for the Dons' third round Uefa Cup tie as Pittodrie was covered with a thin layer of snow. Aberdeen set about upsetting the Germans from the outset and had it not been for some naive decisions, the Dons would have taken a better margin than the 3-2 victory to Germany for the return.

SATURDAY 26TH NOVEMBER 1904

Aberdeen won their first trophy beating Renton 2-0 at Dens Park to lift the Scottish Qualifying Cup. A special Caledonian train left bedecked in the black and gold colours of Aberdeen which took around 600 supporters to the game. There were around 1,500 Dons fans in the crowd of 10,000 for the final. On an ice-bound surface, both sides struggled with the conditions underfoot. A change of boots by all of the Aberdeen players at the interval had the desired effect and two goals from George McNicol brought the cup to Pittodrie.

SATURDAY 26TH NOVEMBER 1983

Gordon Strachan was fast becoming the hottest property around as Real Madrid were the latest side interested in signing him. The Aberdeen midfielder was at his best as the Dons defeated Dundee United 2-0 at Tannadice, scoring a superb second goal as he rounded Narey and McAlpine to score from an acute angle.

SUNDAY 26TH NOVEMBER 1995

Aberdeen won the League Cup for the fifth time after a 2-0 win over Dundee at Hampden Park. Goals from Billy Dodds and Duncan Shearer in each half made sure of a comfortable afternoon for Aberdeen against a Dundee side that were still in the First Division. Stephen Glass was the sponsors' man-of-the-match, picking up a new bicycle for his efforts. Roy Aitken celebrated his first trophy as a manager.

MONDAY 27TH NOVEMBER 1972

A classic League Cup tie as Aberdeen went down 3-2 to Celtic after twice going ahead in their semi-final at Hampden. The 39,682 crowd were treated to both sides pushing for the win. After Dave Robb headed a Varga corner past Williams to put Aberdeen 2-1 ahead, the Dons thought they had done it. An offside-looking Jimmy Johnstone levelled before Callaghan put Celtic ahead in 80 minutes. A late effort from Ian Taylor was saved by Williams as Aberdeen went down fighting.

SATURDAY 28TH NOVEMBER 1964

After a poor start to the season, Aberdeen recovered to take eight points from five games after a convincing 3-0 win at struggling Dundee United. The 6,000 crowd saw Tommy Morrison score for the Dons – his fifth in as many matches – and despite the final score, it was Aberdeen goalkeeper John Ogston who was busier on the day.

SATURDAY 29TH NOVEMBER 1969

The Harper-Forrest double act contrived to dump out Kilmarnock in a 2-0 win at Rugby Park. Killie had just returned from a long European trip to Bulgaria and Aberdeen took full advantage in the latter stages.

THURSDAY 29TH NOVEMBER 2007

A nostalgic trip for a huge Aberdeen following as 7,000 of the Red Army travelled to Madrid for the Dons' Uefa Cup tie against Atletico. The game evoked memories of the Dons' 1983 European Cup Winners' Cup win over arch rivals Real Madrid. The Dons of 2007 could not match those standards and were beaten 2-0 by one of the tournament favourites in the Group B tie.

SATURDAY 30TH NOVEMBER 1968

Disaster for Aberdeen as their season threatened to collapse after a humiliating defeat at Dunfermline Athletic. The home side showed little sign of fatigue from their European exploits and despite a goal from Tommy Craig, the Dons were dealt a hammer blow in a 5-1 defeat. With three wins from their last 11 games, Aberdeen were in relegation trouble…

ABERDEEN FC
On This Day

DECEMBER

SATURDAY 1st DECEMBER 1962

After 14 matches, Aberdeen remained in contention at the top after a 3-1 win over Clyde at Shawfield. The 'Bully Wee' looked destined for relegation as the Dons eased to a comfortable win despite falling behind to a Harry Hood header in eight minutes. Aberdeen were now only three points behind Rangers at the top of the league.

WEDNESDAY 2nd DECEMBER 1902

Representatives of Aberdeen, Orion and Victoria United met for the first time in the County Hotel to discuss the issue of amalgamation to form one club that would compete in the Scottish League. George Alexander of Orion pushed forward the motion and all three clubs were urged to gauge interest among their members. This was seen as the first positive step towards the amalgamation. The Aberdeen clubs were told by the authorities that there was little or no chance that an Aberdeen club would be admitted to the league unless the three main clubs pooled their resources.

SATURDAY 2nd DECEMBER 1939

Tommy Pearson made history when he became the first Scot to play for England. The Newcastle United winger had been taking his seat in the stand at St James' Park when he was summoned by one of the Newcastle directors who told Tommy he was playing – for England! Eric Brooks, a regular in the England side, had been delayed in a car crash so Pearson lined up and helped them to a 2-1 win. Pearson was later capped for Scotland and also went on to play for, and manage, Aberdeen.

WEDNESDAY 2nd DECEMBER 1987

Alex McLeish was captain of Scotland for what was his 50th Scotland appearance, against Luxembourg, in the Stada de la Frontiere. In an almost surreal atmosphere Scotland struggled to break down their hosts and they had to settle for a 0-0 draw before a poor crowd of only 1,999. McLeish went on to become the most capped Aberdeen player in the Dons' history.

SATURDAY 3RD DECEMBER 1966

Aberdeen made it an impressive eight wins in succession to move up to third place in the league after a 2-1 win over Motherwell at Pittodrie. Jimmy Wilson was the Dons hero with both goals in the second half. Aberdeen got over their disappointment in the League Cup to draw level on 20 points with Rangers after 13 games played.

TUESDAY 4TH DECEMBER 1990

The only player to receive two testimonial matches from Aberdeen in modern times was captain Willie Miller. His 20-year service was recognised when a capacity 23,000 crowd turned out to see Miller for the last time as a player. A World XI defeated Aberdeen 5-2 in a match that saw the likes of Charlie Nicholas, Kenny Dalglish, Bruce Grobbelaar, Mark Hughes and Bryan Robson turn out to honour the Aberdeen captain.

SATURDAY 5TH DECEMBER 1970

Aberdeen warmed up for their top-of-the-table clash against Celtic with an emphatic 7-0 win over Cowdenbeath. The Fifers were sadly out of their depth in the top division. Joe Harper scored three but was almost upstaged by Cowdenbeath centre-half Andy Kinnell who put through his own goal on two occasions.

WEDNESDAY 6TH DECEMBER 1967

The first real test for Aberdeen in Europe came against Belgian side Standard Liege. The Belgians had won the first leg of the European Cup Winners' Cup tie 3-0 and had reached the last four of all three European competitions in the past and seemed to have too much experience for Aberdeen. Despite a severe snowstorm that kept the crowd down to 13,000, the Dons, playing in all-white, set about Liege in the return. Goals from Frank Munro and Harry Melrose set up a frantic closing spell as the Dons threw everything at a clearly rattled Liege side. The 2-0 win was not enough their first foray into Europe was over.

SATURDAY 6TH DECEMBER 1975

Rangers long-standing unbeaten record at Pittodrie was finally ended after a stirring Aberdeen performance in their 1-0 win over the Ibrox side. Drew Jarvie scored the only goal of the game in the 83rd minute, to the delight of the 19,600 in attendance. It was also a fantastic start for new Aberdeen captain Willie Miller. John McMaster took advantage of a mix up between Colin Jackson and Rangers goalkeeper Peter McCloy to set up the winner for Jarvie.

SATURDAY 7TH DECEMBER 1901

Aberdeen went clear at the top of the Northern League after a 3-2 win over Orion at Cattofield. Orion, along with Forfar Athletic, were challenging Aberdeen for the championship. The Dons stretched their lead at the top with 16 points from 11 games while Victoria United defeated Forfar 2-1 at Station Park.

SATURDAY 8TH DECEMBER 1979

Aberdeen lost the opportunity to win the League Cup after being held to a dull 0-0 draw against Dundee United at Hampden Park. Despite dominating the game, chances were missed as United adopted a safety first policy that made the final instantly forgettable. Aberdeen had already knocked out both Celtic and Rangers on the way to Hampden as United, by contrast, had not met Premier opposition until the final. The best chance of the game fell to Willie Garner, but his header rolled along the goal line in the Hampden mud. The Dons lost the replay at Dens Park four days later.

SATURDAY 8TH DECEMBER 1984

Eight players were booked as Aberdeen defeated Celtic 4-2 at Pittodrie. It all started when Celtic's Frank McGarvey followed through on Jim Leighton in 24 minutes. Several Aberdeen players were involved as McGarvey sought refuge from referee Young. In between the flying tackles, the Dons carved out chances. Eric Black, then Stewart McKimmie, had fired their side two goals ahead at the interval.

TUESDAY 9TH DECEMBER 1884

Alex Mutch, the Aberdeen goalkeeper, was born in Inverary. Also known as Sandy he made his debut against Hibernian on 18th August 1906. Mutch was transferred to Huddersfield Town in 1910 for a fee of £400 and it was in England that he played in two FA Cup Finals; in 1920 and again in 1922. Mutch joined Newcastle United in 1922 for a fee of £850 and went on to become a groundsman with the Toon after he retired from playing.

SATURDAY 9TH DECEMBER 1972

Joe Harper was sold to Everton for £172,000 amid howls of derision from the Aberdeen support as news of the transfer was announced in the stadium before the start of the visit from Arbroath. Harper had been an Aberdeen talisman ever since his move to the club in 1969. The Dons went on to draw 0-0 with lowly Arbroath as the directors were the target of abuse from a section of the support at the full-time whistle.

WEDNESDAY 9TH DECEMBER 1981

The Dons' Uefa Cup dream ended in the Volkspark Stadium in Hamburg as Aberdeen went down 3-1 in the second leg of their European tie. Taking a 3-2 lead to Germany was always going to be a tough task, and after Hrubesch put Hamburg ahead on away goals, there was no way back for the Dons. Mark McGhee scored a late goal to give his side Dons some hope, but they were left to curse their late mistakes in the first game in Scotland.

SATURDAY 10TH DECEMBER 1927

Ireland centre-half Eddie Falloon made his Aberdeen debut in the 2-2 draw against Cowdenbeath at Central Park. Falloon went on to play 249 games for the Dons and was capped by Northern Ireland. Falloon also had the honour of being captain in the club's first Scottish Cup Final in 1937.

WEDNESDAY 11TH DECEMBER 2002

Aberdeen turned to Inverness manager Steve Paterson to replace Ebbe Skovdahl as boss. Paterson's appointment was hastened after the Dane declared that he would be leaving Aberdeen at the end of that season. Paterson arrived after a poor spell under Skovdahl had not taken the club forward as expected, despite heavy investment being made in the squad. Steve Paterson was never afforded such riches and his record of bargain hunting in the lower divisions was one of the reasons he was favoured by Aberdeen. It all ended in embarrassment in May 2004 when Paterson left Aberdeen in the boot of an official's car to avoid the gathered media!

SATURDAY 12TH DECEMBER 1970

Billed as a league decider so early in the season, both Aberdeen and Celtic were so far ahead of the chasing pack that only the Dons could catch the Parkhead side. A huge crowd of 63,000 turned out for the clash of the top two, but they were silenced when Aberdeen scored the winning goal in 53 minutes. A classic long throw from Jim Hermiston was flicked on by Dave Robb. Joe Harper escaped the attentions of Billy McNeill to head past Fallon. Despite a relentless siege by the home side, the Aberdeen defence held out without conceding a goal for the seventh game in succession.

WEDNESDAY 13TH DECEMBER 1978

The Aberdeen support in the 21,050 crowd found it hard to believe that the Dons had to go to extra time to see off the stubborn resistance of Hibernian in their League Cup semi-final at Dens Park. It took a speculative lob from Stuart Kennedy to finally beat Hibs goalkeeper MacDonald, who had kept his side in the tie with a succession of saves. The Dons were through to their fourth League Cup Final after Kennedy's goal in 106 minutes.

JOE HARPER HEADS THE DONS' WINNER AGAINST CELTIC IN DECEMBER 1970

SATURDAY 13TH DECEMBER 1980

Ian Angus made his first start for the Dons as Rangers were once again humbled before 20,000 fans at Pittodrie. Mark McGhee scored the opening goal and Pittodrie erupted in the final minute when Rangers' Derek Johnstone put through his own net.

WEDNESDAY 14TH DECEMBER 1988

Alex McLeish was rewarded for his long service to Aberdeen with a glamour testimonial at Pittodrie. A capacity all-ticket 23,000 crowd were treated to an exhibition game between the Aberdeen Gothenburg XI and an international-select side. McLeish scored twice in a diplomatic 3-3 draw. Also on show was ageing rock star Rod Stewart who showed he was not wasting his time as an apprentice with Brentford all those years ago. Kenny Dalglish also played alongside current Dons Jim Bett and Paul Mason in the international select side.

SATURDAY 15TH DECEMBER 1951

Aberdeen played with a white ball for the first time when Morton visited Pittodrie on league duty. Previously, the older brown leather balls were preferred but with the dark winter afternoons setting in, and in the days before floodlights, the new white balls were an immediate success with both players and supporters.

SATURDAY 15TH DECEMBER 1956

Brockville was a mud heap as conditions for the visit of Aberdeen deteriorated as the game went on. It didn't prevent the Dons hitting five goals in a 5-2 win that was the third in succession. The players from both sides had to change their strips at half-time as neither was distinguishable from the mud-spattered shirts.

SUNDAY 15TH DECEMBER 2002

Steve Paterson's first game in charge was a disaster for Aberdeen as they went down 3-0 to Dunfermline Athletic. After Ebbe Skovdahl announced he was leaving, the club moved swiftly to appoint Inverness manager Paterson and his assistant Duncan Shearer in an effort to revive fortunes.

THURSDAY 16TH DECEMBER 1971

Scott Booth, the Scotland international, was born in Aberdeen. Booth emerged from the successful Aberdeen youth side of 1989 and also established himself in the Scotland side. In 1997, he completed a shock move to Borussia Dortmund which left the Dons without any transfer fee. Six years later, after another spell in Holland, Booth returned to Pittodrie under new manager Steve Paterson.

THURSDAY 17TH DECEMBER 1908

Tom Niblo was signed from Aston Villa after some lengthy negotiations by Aberdeen manager Jimmy Philip. Niblo was seen as a significant addition to the team having been capped for Scotland against England in 1904. Philip also secured the signing of Bert Murray that week. The club had been criticised for the quality of new signings in recent years, but Niblo was a welcome addition.

TUESDAY 18TH DECEMBER 1906

Irish international Charlie O'Hagan signed for Aberdeen from Middlesbrough. It was seen as a coup to attract a player of such quality. O'Hagan was a seasoned international and went on become the first Aberdeen player to play for his country. He was also made captain of Ireland during his spell with the Dons after spending time with Tottenham Hotspur earlier in his career.

FRIDAY 18TH DECEMBER 1964

Charlie Cooke, the Dons winger, and hero of the support, was sold to Dundee in a surprise transfer. Although the Dens Park club paid £44,000, the Aberdeen fans were aghast that he was allowed to join a club of Dundee's stature. The belief was that Cooke was destined to join a big club in England; that move did materialise some two years later when he joined Chelsea. The following day, as Aberdeen were beaten 3-0 at home to Clyde, manager Tommy Pearson appeared on the track side and was roundly jeered by the 3,000 crowd.

SUNDAY 19TH DECEMBER 2004

A sad day for Aberdeen as a memorial service to remember Hicham Zerouali was held at Pittodrie. Zerouali was a popular player with the Dons and his sudden death in a road accident in Morocco came as a huge shock for all connected with the club.

TUESDAY 20TH DECEMBER 1983

Aberdeen defeated European Cup Winners SV Hamburg 2-0 at Pittodrie to win the European Super Cup. Goals from Mark McGhee and Neil Simpson in the second period proved decisive after a 0-0 draw in Germany. Aberdeen became the only Scottish side to be crowned Super Cup winners in a game that was beamed live to more than 80 countries worldwide.

THURSDAY 20TH DECEMBER 2008

In the Dons' final Group B Uefa Cup match against Copenhagen, a 4-0 win against the Danes put Aberdeen through to the knockout stages for the first time in their history. In a tough group that also included Atletico Madrid, Panathinaikos and Lokomotiv Moscow, two goals from Jamie Smith put Aberdeen through to the last 32.

SATURDAY 21ST DECEMBER 1907

After joing the Dons from Middlesbrough in May, Tom Murray scored in seven successive league matches – a record – the last of which came in the 1-0 win over Hearts at Pittodrie. Murray set a new club record of 19 goals in his first season. After a short spell with Rangers he returned to Pittodrie before being sold to Hearts in 1911.

SATURDAY 22ND DECEMBER 1906

Irish international Charlie O'Hagan made his debut for Aberdeen against Rangers at Pittodrie. O'Hagan was seen as a huge signing for the club who had been criticised in recent months for not strengthening the team. O'Hagan went on to form a partnership with Willie Lennie that brought the club close to winning their first title in 1908. O'Hagan went on to captain Ireland against Scotland where he came up against his Aberdeen team-mate.

SATURDAY 22ND DECEMBER 1956

After three wins in a row, the Dons went down 3-1 at home to Motherwell. The visitors were in second place in the table and despite Harry Yorston putting Aberdeen ahead after four minutes, Motherwell hit back after the Dons lost Jimmy Mitchell, who was taken to hospital with a shoulder injury. The only thing that could have saved Aberdeen was the famous North Sea haar which threatened to force abandonment at one stage.

SATURDAY 23RD DECEMBER 1911

Scotland winger Willie Lennie rescued a point for Aberdeen in a 1-1 draw against Hibernian at Easter Road. The Dons had been struggling to reach the high of finishing in second place the previous season. Aberdeen had been successful on their travels that season but it was their home form that had left them struggling in mid-table.

SATURDAY 23RD DECEMBER 1961

Defending champions Rangers were confident that lowly Aberdeen would be no trouble for them at Ibrox but the Dons went ahead after only 20 seconds when the ball came off Jim Baxter, and Ken Brownlee put the visitors ahead. George Kinnell celebrated his 24th birthday with a trademark penalty after Eric Caldow punched the ball off the line. The Dons went on to win 4-2 before a 28,000 crowd.

SATURDAY 24TH DECEMBER 1977

With Aberdeen the only challengers to Rangers for the league title, it was a crucial game for the Dons that they simply had to win to keep in touch at the top of the table. There was little Christmas spirit on show as a frantic match enjoyed its fair share of controversy. The all-ticket 21,000 crowd were in raptures as Aberdeen hit Rangers for four with Joe Harper and Dave Robb among the goals. Even a small pitch invasion by Blues' supporters after the Dons' third goal failed to take the shine off what was a superb performance from Aberdeen.

FRIDAY 25TH DECEMBER 1908

Goals from Tom Niblo and Sandy McNair gave Aberdeen a 2-2 win over Falkirk at Pittodrie before a crowd of 5,000. The game was a North-Eastern Cup semi-final and Aberdeen fielded their entire first team for the game despite having to play Queen's Park in Glasgow in a Division One match 24 hours later.

SATURDAY 25TH DECEMBER 1909

Aberdeen made the long trip down to Airdrie and came away with a 3-1 win after goals from Miller, Simpson and Lennie kept the Dons in control against the Broomfield side. The reserves were also enjoying the winning habit as back at Pittodrie they crushed Banff 6-0 to progress in the Aberdeenshire Cup.

THURSDAY 25TH DECEMBER 1947

Harry Yorston and Archie Kelly made their first-team debuts for Aberdeen as the Dons went down 3-1 to Third Lanark at Cathkin Park. Aberdeen had been struggling in the league and had just sold George Hamilton to Hearts with Kelly and £7,000 coming the other way. Despite Yorston scoring on his debut, Aberdeen were back in the relegation mix after bottom club Third's surprise win.

SATURDAY 25TH DECEMBER 1965

It was a miserable Christmas for Aberdeen as they lost 3-1 at home to Hibernian. Three goals after the interval from the Easter Road side ensured that the Eddie Turnbull revolution was put on hold. The Aberdeen manager could not inspire his side to take anything against the club where he made his name as a player. Ernie Winchester came close on two occasions as the Dons continued to press without success.

SATURDAY 26TH DECEMBER 1953

Aberdeen registered their highest win since the war with an emphatic 8-0 hammering of struggling Stirling Albion at Pittodrie. This Boxing Day clash was a real knockout for the 15,000 supporters. For once, George Hamilton missed out in the goals as all the other Aberdeen forwards helped to increase the Dons' goal difference.

SATURDAY 26TH DECEMBER 1959

A Boxing Day feast for Aberdeen supporters as the Dons defeated third-placed Hibernian 6-4 at Pittodrie. Despite going two goals behind, Aberdeen responded in style, hitting six, which was far removed from their previous form. Jackie Hather was playing in an unfamiliar inside-forward role and was inspired in front of the 15,000 crowd.

SATURDAY 27TH DECEMBER 1980

The unlikely pairing of McLeish and Miller scored in the opening period to put Aberdeen on their way to a 4-1 success over Celtic at Pittodrie before an all-ticket 24,000 crowd. The win put Aberdeen three points ahead at the top with a game in hand. Gordon Strachan's penalty in 69 minutes put the Dons four goals ahead before Charlie Nicholas pulled one back for the visitors. The victory rounded off a superb year for Aberdeen after winning the title in May.

FRIDAY 28TH DECEMBER 1906

Fixture chaos hit Aberdeen as the severe storms caused havoc with the club's plans. With games to be played at Heart of Midlothian, St Mirren and Falkirk in the space of five days, Aberdeen decided to set up base at Bridge of Allan. The severe weather caused widespread disruption all over the country and the Aberdeen party were told that the train line was blocked at Fourdon so travel was impossible.

The situation had not been resolved by the next morning and despite their best efforts, the club were unable to make it to Edinburgh for the Hearts game. It was more of the same for the visit to Paisley as the team were unable to get past Dunblane and the weary Aberdeen party arrived too late for the game to go ahead. To round off a miserable period for the Dons they were fined by the SFA for failing to fulfil their obligations!

SATURDAY 28TH DECEMBER 1963

A troubled year came to a close as Aberdeen were humbled 5-0 at home to Partick Thistle. Two goals just before the interval ended the Dons' chances as the visitors eased to their first away win of the season. It was the worst possible start to a hectic festive schedule for the club. Nevertheless the Dons won 4-1 at Dundee 24 hours later.

SATURDAY 29TH DECEMBER 1951

Celtic arrived at Pittodrie in the bottom half of the league but defeated Aberdeen in a classic 4-3 win before a 22,500 crowd. Don Emery was the Aberdeen sinner, giving away two penalties, both of which were despatched by Bobby Collins. Aberdeen were trailing 4-1 with seven minutes left and a late rally almost brought them a point as Don Emery and Harry Yorston scored in the closing minutes.

SATURDAY 30TH DECEMBER 1961

Charlie Nicholas of Celtic, Arsenal and Aberdeen was born in Glasgow. Nicholas emerged in the Celtic side in the early 1980s as a player of real potential. After being sold to Arsenal in 1984, it was Ian Porterfield that brought him to Pittodrie in the New Year of 1988. His first appearance at Pittodrie drew a 20,000 crowd for the visit of Dunfermline Athetic. Nicholas parted company with Aberdeen immediately after scoring one of the penalties that won the Scottish Cup in 1990 as the Dons defeated his old club.

SATURDAY 31ST DECEMBER 1910

A hammer blow to Aberdeen's championship hopes as they went down 2-0 against St Mirren in Paisley. Despite Tom Murray hitting the post and Pat Travers going close on two occasions, it was not to be for Aberdeen before a 7,000 crowd. Back at Pittodrie, the Aberdeen reserves hit seven without reply against Partick Thistle 'A' in front of 1,500 fans in a reserve league fixture.

SATURDAY 31ST DECEMBER 1960

Aberdeen ended 1960 with a real flourish as they beat Dunfermline Athletic 6-2 at East End Park. Ken Brownlee was the Aberdeen hero with four goals as the Dons avenged an opening day defeat against the Pars and slipped into second place in the table behind Rangers.